Introduction to
Dyslexia

Introduction to Dyslexia

Lindsay Peer
and Gavin Reid

David Fulton Publishers
London

David Fulton Publishers Ltd
The Chiswick Centre, 414 Chiswick High Road, London W4 5TF

www.fultonpublishers.co.uk

David Fulton Publishers is a division of Granada Media Limited, part of the Granada Media group.

First published 2003
10 9 8 7 6 5 4 3 2 1

British Library Cataloguing in Publication Data
A Catalogue record for this book is available from the British Library.

ISBN 1 85346 964 5

Typeset by Pracharak Technologies (P) Ltd, Madras, India
Printed and bound in Great Britain by Ashford Colour Press Limited, Gosport, Hants

Contents

About the authors

Lindsay Peer CBE is Education Director and Deputy Chief Executive of the British Dyslexia Association. She is a widely recognised authority in the field of dyslexia and mainstream education. She appears regularly at national and international events, and has published a considerable body of material, both theoretical and practical. She has written, edited and contributed to many books on dyslexia for parents and teachers. Together with Dr Gavin Reid, she co-edited the books *Multilingualism, Literacy and Dyslexia: A Challenge for Educators* (2000) and *Dyslexia: Successful Inclusion in the Secondary School* (2001), both published by David Fulton.

Dr Peer's field of experience covers teacher training, research and the teaching of both mainstream students and those with Specific Learning Difficulties/Dyslexia from preschool through to adult education. She spent 20 years as a classroom teacher and is Vice-Chair of the British Dyslexia Association's Accreditation Board, working closely with higher education institutions. She also has considerable experience of educational needs assessment and counselling, and is particularly interested in the teaching of English as an Additional Language, and specific skills relating to the educational development of bilingual students with learning problems.

Lindsay Peer's work involves close liaison with various government departments both in the UK and abroad, including the Department for Education and Skills, the Teacher Training Agency and the Qualifications and Curriculum Authority. Among the committees of which she is a member is the National Literacy and Numeracy Strategy Group. She has given evidence to House of Commons Select Committees.

In addition to her BDA work, between September 2001 and August 2002, Dr Peer acted as Senior Consultant for the project, 'Leading for Inclusion' at the National College for School Leadership. She was awarded a CBE in the 2002 New Years Honours List, and is a Fellow of the Royal Society of Arts. She is a member of the International Academy for Research in Learning Disabilities. She has also been awarded a PhD by the Psychology Department of the University of Sheffield.

Gavin Reid is Senior Lecturer in Educational Studies at the Moray House School of Education, University of Edinburgh. He is an experienced teacher, educational psychologist, university lecturer, author and researcher. He has lectured internationally in many countries throughout Europe, New Zealand, Asia, eastern Europe and the United States. He has authored and edited key course books for teacher training in the field of dyslexia and literacy. *Dyslexia: A Practitioner's Handbook* (2nd edn), published by Wiley, has been used as a course text in many university and college courses on dyslexia worldwide, and together with Lindsay Peer, he has edited the books *Dyslexia: Successful Inclusion in the Secondary School* and *Multilingualism, Literacy and Dyslexia*, both published by David Fulton Publishers. He has also co-authored two assessment packages with Dr Charles Weedon, a group test in literacy development – *Listening and Literacy Index* – and a computer-aided diagnostic and profiling kit for specific learning difficulties – SNAP – both published by Hodder and Stoughton. He has also co-authored, with Jane Kirk, the book *Dyslexia in Adults*, and has co-edited with Janice Wearmouth the book *Dyslexia and Literacy* (both published by Wiley), which is the set book for the Open University/University of Edinburgh course on difficulties in literacy development. He has co-authored the book *Meeting Difficulties in Literacy Development: Research, Policy and Practice* with Janice Wearmouth and Janet Soler (published by Routledge 2003).

Dr Reid has taught in secondary schools and has worked as an education authority educational psychologist. He developed the first Master's course in dyslexia in the UK in 1992. The course was also prepared in an open learning format, and has since been further developed in association with the Open University. The result of this collaboration between the Open University and the University of Edinburgh is the postgraduate Award in Difficulties in Literacy Development, which commenced in October 2002, being run by both the OU and the University of Edinburgh. He is a consultant to a number of national and international projects on dyslexia and is a consultant to the Red Rose School for students with specific learning difficulties in St Annes-on-Sea, Lancashire, England. He currently holds appointments as external examiner to universities in Scotland, England and Australia, and is a member of the British Dyslexia Association Teacher Training Accreditation Board having worked as a consultant to many parent groups and charitable bodies in the UK, Europe and New Zealand.

Preface

This book is the introduction to the series on Inclusion in the Secondary School to be published by David Fulton Publishers. The series will include a number of books written by subject teachers and those involved in the field of dyslexia. The area of accessing the full curriculum and assisting students with dyslexia to reach their full potential has been seen as a considerable challenge for secondary school teachers. The demands of the subject-orientated syllabus and the pace of preparation for examinations has resulted in many students with dyslexia underachieving and many teachers becoming frustrated. For some time now the needs of students with dyslexia has been seen as the responsibility of specialist teachers. While there is a clear role for those who have a specialism and extended training in dyslexia, it is suggested here that the key role in supporting students with dyslexia should be in the hands of the subject teacher in secondary schools and the class teacher in primary schools. Supporting students with dyslexia involves more than helping students in class; it also requires a focus on curriculum planning, learning and teaching styles, subject differentiation, examination reappraisal and whole-school staff development.

It is hoped that this book and the forthcoming series will facilitate these developments and provide subject teachers with the information and guidance they need to have the confidence and the knowledge to support students with dyslexia in all subjects.

The book that precedes this series, *Dyslexia: Successful Inclusion in the Secondary School*, edited by Lindsay Peer and Gavin Reid, has been warmly welcomed by subject teachers and this current series is seen as a follow up to that book. The series will provide detailed examination of different subject areas in a user-friendly format that can become a useful source for subject teachers who may have little previous knowledge of dyslexia.

We are extremely fortunate in working with, and having the agreement of many subject specialists who will be contributing to this series. We recognise that their contribution will be welcomed and will be a significant contribution in the process of full curriculum

at dyslexia is, and how it is
also highlight how it can affect
s the social and emotional
dyslexia. While awareness has
years, there is still some
causes of dyslexia and the
and practice.

the individual concerned, but
hat dyslexia will not disappear,
will help overcome difficulties
videly noted that many people
lls in areas such as problem-
well as skills with computers. It
pport are age- and interest-
n dyslexia may be behind their
lls, at various stages in both
y may be ahead in terms of
ay this understanding orally or

he learning needs of dyslexic
ges of their lives. From the stage
he assessment and provision
vill be involved – all requiring
g and development. This book
assessment strategies and tests
the need for effective classroom
cted in isolation but needs to be
d task outcomes.

ctive teaching and learning will
deed, throughout the series. It is
nption that as long as the learner
s learning. This may not be the
is indeed one of the reasons for
aign, the issuing of Awareness
he general enhancement of the
oms and schools, primary and

access for students with dyslexia. It is hoped that, through this, many students with dyslexia will, in fact, fulfil their potential, and that this will help them to develop the confidence and the means to experience success in secondary school, in further and higher education and in the workplace.

Lindsay Peer CBE
Gavin Reid
December 2002

About the book

In this book, we will describe
manifested in the classroom. We
the home environment as we
development of the young person
been raised substantially over
misconception about the underl
influence of these in relation to p

Dyslexia is a lifelong challeng
while there is a need to acknowled
skills and strategies can be taught
and develop strengths. It has bee
with dyslexia have considerable
solving, creativity, art and design,
is important that materials and
appropriate, as although learners
peers in reading and/or writing
primary and secondary school t
understanding and may have to di
visually for it to be acknowledged.

It is now well understood tha
people change at various ages and s
of initial identification, through
processes, a range of practitioners
different levels of awareness, trair
will therefore discuss the types o
available to teachers, which include
observation. Assessment is not con
linked to curriculum development a

The need for an evaluation of ef
also be discussed in this book and,
too easy to make the misguided ass
with dyslexia is in the class, he/she
case, especially in a large class. Thi
the Dyslexia-Friendly Schools cam
Packs (BDA 1999) to schools and
awareness of dyslexia in all class
secondary, throughout the country.

Dyslexia-friendly schools

Undoubtedly, the introduction of this concept, with its unique way of working is an innovation that has made a great deal of difference to the lives of many people. The principle of working towards the facilitation of all people to reach their educational potential – regardless of challenge or disability – is fundamental to the principle of 'dyslexia-friendliness'. It is fully recognised that it is only when a head teacher and senior management team lead the way for such changes in attitude that teachers feel empowered, parents feel confident and children become successful.

People with dyslexia have a great deal to offer society. Their creativity, skills and talents which so often lie dormant within a framework of frustration may not be helped by a traditional educational environment. A dyslexia-friendly environment and appropriate support will open doors for those who hitherto may have experienced failure. Primarily, there needs to be a change of attitude within the learning environment – an attitude that is shared by all members of staff and echoed by school peers.

Features of dyslexia-friendly schools

In order to make sure that dyslexia-friendly schools become a reality, clear written guidelines need to be produced for teachers which ensure that the needs of dyslexic learners are an integral part of the whole-school policy. This should enable them to develop strengths at the same time as addressing their weaknesses. Furthermore, school management should ideally 'buy into' the concept and ensure that all staff are working within the philosophy of a dyslexia-friendly school.

Schools need to adopt an open and flexible approach, encouraging communication between all parties. This would include external agencies where appropriate, in addition to staff and pupils them-selves. High, yet realistic, expectations of all learners must be demanded. Policies and alternative methodologies will encourage the self-esteem of children who find learning through traditional methodologies frustrating. There also needs to be recognition of the needs of those dyslexic learners entering the education system with a background of more than one language. Schools should encourage specialist teachers and speech and language therapists working in an advisory capacity to make regular visits to schools to evaluate, support and advise on how to improve provision. Whole-school approaches ensure that policies are translated into action. Comprehensive and appropriate training for different levels of staff needs to be provided together with an agreement that all staff are responsible for the progress of each individual learner. Schools should be encouraged to monitor and evaluate their work and the system as a whole. Teaching of study skills, learning styles and thinking skills would be ideally suited to all children in such a school. By doing so, standards across the board have been seen to rise. Parents should be helped to be positive in their support both of individual children and the school. This will often happen when they feel that their children are receiving support and understanding and progress is clearly being made. Particular note and consideration should also be made of the needs of those from cultures where priorities may not be with the learning of English as a primary language.

Individual target-setting should be aimed at the level where learners are, rather than at where they should be according to age. Furthermore, recognition of and support geared to intellectual potential rather than level of difficulties should be the focus. Multi-sensory teaching methodologies to enhance learning capabilities are of great value to learners with dyslexia. For those with more severe needs, the introduction of programmes to enhance development of those areas underlying dyslexic weaknesses – e.g. speed of processing, memory, language, organisation – will be invaluable. All staff, regardless of subject specialism, should share the responsibility for each individual.

Ethnic minority learners

Identifying the literacy and communication needs of multilingual children in a culture-fair manner will not only help to ensure the preservation of different cultures but will also help to identify the cognitive abilities and communication skills of multilingual children.

It is necessary that culture-fair principles and practices are considered in the identification and assessment processes, in classroom practices and provision, the curriculum, in the training of teachers, support assistants and psychologists, in the selection and allocation of resources, in policy and in liaison with parents and the wider community. The need to maximise the potential of dyslexic learners whose first language may not be English is of paramount importance and this must be the priority in the development and implementation of identification and assessment procedures.

Young people who are bi-/multilingual and dyslexic have a learning profile which is significantly different to that of their peers. Educators are often aware that these students are very different from others who experience difficulty, as they are often bright and 'able', orally or visually. The difference between their abilities and the low level of written work they produce can, but not always, be glaringly obvious.

Culture-free testing needs to be used as well as specially developed reading materials. Without the awareness of different learning and socialising habits of the particular culture from which the child comes, many unfortunate assumptions may be made about the child's assumed lack of ability. Tests given orally are prone to bias and therefore have to be considered with great care and knowledge on the part of the tester.

It is not a viable proposition to trust the use of translation for administration of tests for children whose native language is not the language in which the tests were designed. There may be problems of cultural and linguistic bias, differing syntax and structure, which would make them unreliable, hence any results can be invalid. Materials developed for assessment and teaching need to acknowledge the diversity of communities and of individuals within these communities.

Avenues for effective communication necessitate openness to ensure the effective triangular working partnerships of parents, schools and the individual children concerned. There are still communities in which dyslexia is misunderstood and for whom awareness and understanding need to be raised. Until such times, success is likely to be limited. This greater understanding needs to be accepted and acted upon by policy-makers nationally and locally in individual schools.

The McPherson Report (1999) suggested that every institution should examine their policies and the outcomes of these policies in order to ensure that no section of any community is placed at a disadvantage. This should include the dyslexic community in its entirety. Information needs to be dispersed throughout the communities in relation to dyslexia, and avenues need to be opened for parents of dyslexic children as well as dyslexic adults in order to allay fears and encourage communication. Like the parents of monolingual dyslexic children, parents from bi- and multilingual communities need to be trained in self-advocacy and to participate in groups designed to influence policy and practice.

Challenging behaviour and dyslexia

Frustration leads, very often, to antisocial or even deviant behaviour. There is no doubt that the strain placed on children to 'do better' when they are already trying to do their best is unreasonable. Often the child's problems are attributed to emotional issues, sometimes with a background of difficulties at home. It is the responsibility of educators to look for the root causes of the stress; after all, even the most effective form of counselling will not help the child whose underlying difficulties have not been identified and addressed. We know of many anecdotes about children displaying significant behavioural problems related to frustration, who seem to improve dramatically when the situation, that is inappropriate, is replaced by a more suitable structured environment. One such case was Steven, a bilingual dyslexic boy, aged 13, who had experienced major problems, both academic and social, at school. He was labelled hyperactive. His behaviour was so poor that he was eventually sent to a special school where, within five months, there were no signs of 'hyperactivity'. On discussion with his class teacher, a year later, she was amazed to hear that there had ever been any behavioural problems. However, the parents were deeply saddened that this had been the only solution for their son whom they wished to have raised at home and not just visit at a boarding school at weekends.

Hyperactivity

On an everyday basis we see children who may be extremely difficult in some classes, yet not in others. We may not consider them to be hyperactive, but as educators we do need to be introspective and consider underlying difficulties. Teachers often ask whether it might be the subject matter, the mode of teaching, the learning environment or possibly a personality clash with specific staff that is causing the trouble. Many of these children are simply 'reacting' to the situation in which they find themselves.

Genuine hyperactivity may well start before the child enters school; everyone is aware of it. Sleepless nights and unacceptable behaviour are often part of the report that parents give. For this there are a variety of treatments, which are often a combination of educational and medical interventions. However, there are also children who seem to develop similar behavioural patterns to those who are genuinely hyperactive, but the symptoms only start when things begin to go wrong in the school environment. Interventions in these circumstances are totally different. When placed in a 'dyslexia-friendly' environment, be it either specialist school or mainstream school, with appropriate provision and an empathetic staff, who are knowledgeable and understanding, the 'hyperactivity' often disappears. That is because it was not hyperactivity. As parents and teachers in secondary schools in particular know (the time when hormones hit with a vengeance), questions need to be asked and background information obtained which relate to the child's behaviour and performance in primary school and, in some cases, preschool. Worryingly, there are many children with dyslexia who are admitted to schools for children who are suffering from emotional and behavioural difficulties (EBD). These may well be inappropriate placements.

Bullying

There are groups of children with dyslexia who experience weaknesses in the areas of fine and/or gross motor skills. In the past these children were described as 'clumsy'. Children who have overlapping features of dyslexia and dyspraxia appear to be the ones who are most easily bullied. Such children describe themselves as unwanted in the playground, in the sports hall and in practical workshops within the curriculum. They talk of teachers making unpleasant jibes and children picking up on those comments in the playground. Some are in physical fear of other children.

Teachers need to be working with this group to develop the muscle control, body language and self-esteem that they are lacking. All staff working in a dyslexia-friendly school will be aware of these issues and will look out for them. This needs to be recognised and addressed by changes in national policy and local practice.

Parental stress – a positive outcome

Initially, there is a need to appreciate why it is that parents are often stressed and appear angry with schools. Many parents are themselves dyslexic and for them this is a repetition of the struggles they themselves experienced in school. Often misguided and ill-informed 'help', such as comments like 'Don't worry, he'll grow out of it/ he'll mature', are most unhelpful, as people do not 'grow out' of dyslexia but have to learn to cope with it and use their skills to overcome their difficulties. It is for this reason that subject and career choice is of immense importance and, ideally, careers advisers should have knowledge of dyslexia. This would help them guide the young person with dyslexia into the most appropriate course of study or employment.

Biggar and Barr (1996) showed how when tensions between home and school are evident, the resulting frustration and feelings of failure are often echoed in the child. Homework and disorganisation can also cause tensions at home. Furthermore, as dyslexia tends to be a hereditary difficulty, the chances are that there are others at home who experience similar frustrations and, indeed, may not be able to help the child with homework.

Reassuring parents

Once parents are reassured that the school understands their child and is making appropriate provision for them, tensions reduce radically. Parents hope to see the classroom teacher recognising ability while help is being given for the weaknesses. This will only happen once the strengths and weaknesses have been defined and a solid programme of support is in place. When regular communication follows and there is strong evidence of improvement, life is better for all concerned. It also helps if parents are put in touch with local dyslexia support groups where they can learn more about dyslexia, how to work with the school and how to support the child at home. Action-based support and communication are essential ingredients to a fruitful and positive relationship.

Chapter 2

What is Dyslexia?

Dyslexia is a label, but one than can carry significant weight in terms of resources, examination support, teaching approaches, assessment needs, curriculum differentiation and management, and parental involvement. For those reasons it is important that the class teacher has more than just an awareness of dyslexia, and has instead a sound understanding of the nature of the dyslexic profile underpinning this label, the characteristics of dyslexia and how children and young people with dyslexia can best be supported in all areas of the curriculum.

Characteristics of dyslexia

The most commonly held view and perception of dyslexia is how it relates to difficulties with reading and spelling. These difficulties are in fact readily observable characteristics of dyslexia. Many children, however, display such difficulties in literacy, but not all are dyslexic. It is important, therefore, to present a comprehensive view of the characteristics of dyslexia. An outline of the main characteristics are shown below.

Reading
Children with dyslexia will usually, but not always, have a difficulty with reading. This could be with fluency, that is speed of reading; or accuracy – they may hesitate over words or make a guess based on the anticipated meaning of the word or through utilising the visual features of the word. There may also be a difficulty in reading

comprehension, but this is not due to lack of understanding, rather a result of the difficulties in fluency and reading. Indeed the research suggests that fluency is an important factor in the development of comprehension.

Spelling

Spelling difficulties are often an obvious characteristic of dyslexia. Quite often the word misspelt is a commonly used one, and often there is a pattern of errors, perhaps the 'er', 'ar', 'or' ending of a word or the double vowel sound 'ee', 'ea', 'ei'. Often the sequence of letters can be jumbled.

Writing

Children with dyslexia may also have difficulties in both expressive writing and their actual handwriting style. Expressive writing is an important element in examinations, whether it is factual writing, descriptive or imaginative, the dyslexic student may not perform to his/her real ability. In handwriting, letters may be badly formed with no distinctive style. Also there may be inconsistent use of capital and lower case letters. This type of difficulty is likely to deteriorate in, for example, examinations, which is why examiners should always be alerted to the presence of a dyslexic difficulty. In expressive writing the actual writing piece may not reflect the imaginative ideas and creativity of the dyslexic student. Often dyslexic students can be very creative, but their grammar and perhaps even a lack of access to an extended vocabulary may minimise the presentation of the piece of writing. This can be very frustrating.

Memory

Children with dyslexia often have difficulties in both short-term and long-term memory. This may not always be the case as often they can develop reasonably efficient methods of retaining and recalling information. More often than not, however, the bulk of information to be remembered in some subject areas can prove challenging.

Coordination

Although not all dyslexic children have difficulties in coordination, some have, and this can have implications for practical work in some subjects. The coordination difficulties may be seen in handwriting, other fine motor activities, such as using scissors, and sometimes in general coordination, such as in sport. It is worth stressing, however, that this is not always the case, and some dyslexic children may well have a talent for art and crafts as well as subjects such as physical education and sport.

Organisational difficulties

This is perhaps one of the least obvious but, nevertheless, very important aspects of dyslexia. Organisation is important for all stages of learning, and the material to be learnt has to be organised in the brain – the new material has to be connected to previous learning and concepts have to be developed on the topic being learnt and related to previous learning and existing knowledge. This requires a degree of organisation, and very often this activity takes place in the brain without the learner being aware of it. Children with dyslexia, however, may not be able to relate new learning to that already learnt and often the connections between new and previous learning have to be clearly displayed by the teacher. This cognitive organisational difficulty may not be too obvious to the teacher, but it emphasises the view that dyslexia is more than a reading difficulty; it is associated with learning and information processing.

Information processing

This relates to how we learn new material. Basically there are three overlapping stages: input; cognition and output. The dyslexic learner may have difficulties at any, or all three, stages of this cycle.

The input stage relates to how the information is presented – when we are learning new information the material to be learnt must make some impact on the learner at the crucial initial stage of learning. Material can be presented in a number of ways:

- auditory – through the teacher talking or the pupil listening to a tape;
- visually – through diagrams, videos or some other visual means;
- tactile methods, where the pupil is involved in touching, such as in practical experiments or in technical subjects; and
- kinesthetically – this involves the pupils experiencing learning, for example, through drama, fieldwork, group work and role play.

There is some evidence that dyslexic children may learn more effectively through the visual and kinesthetic modalities as well as through the tactile mode (West 1997). The main point is that the auditory mode, which is probably the modality used most in schools, is the weakest mode for effective learning for dyslexic children.

Phonological difficulties

Perhaps one of the main reasons for the difficulties dyslexic children display in reading and spelling is that of phonological difficulties. This relates to an awareness of sounds and the characteristics of these sounds in words; where in a word sounds appear; and the general rhythm of words. For example, they may have difficulty remembering rhymes and identifying particular sounds in a word. Since the English language is an irregular language with 44 sounds and only 26 letters, it can be appreciated that knowledge of these sounds is important for reading and spelling. It is widely recognised that this difficulty is one of the principal difficulties associated with dyslexia and this can present a particular challenge for teachers in secondary school (as well as in primary) as many of the phonics reading programmes are not age- appropriate for secondary school age children. But, on the other hand, many students with dyslexia have good language experience and can often use contextual cues to predict a word rather than read it through a decoding process.

Visual difficulties

There is also a growing body of evidence indicating that visual factors are associated with dyslexia. This can take the form of visual distortion of letters, blurring, letters merging into each other and missing lines or words when reading. This can have implications for accuracy in reading instructions, for example in laboratory subjects, and in following the sequence of instructions. This difficulty may also be noted in numbers, for example in tables and other forms of data such as graphs.

Discrepancies

One of the defining factors that can be associated with dyslexia is the discrepancies which can be noted in different curricular areas. Very often the young person with dyslexic difficulties can have considerable difficulties in some subject areas, particularly those which are heavily literacy based. At the same time, however, they may display considerable skills in some other subjects, such as art, music or perhaps even English Literature. These discrepancies can sometimes be quite marked and emphasise that dyslexia is a specific difficulty that applies to learning in specific situations. This can result in a dyslexic profile in which significant discrepancies between students' performances in different subject areas are very marked.

One can note, therefore, that there are a number of different characteristics of dyslexia, and it is important that the class teacher not only has some knowledge of dyslexia, but is also provided with sufficient information based on an accurate assessment of the difficulties and the strengths of the student. It is also important that the class teacher is familiar with what dyslexia is, the definition used by the education authority, and how that definition relates to practice.

Definitions of dyslexia

There are a number of definitions of dyslexia currently in use. These can be described as descriptive definitions, working definitions and operational definitions. The British Dyslexia Association definition (Peer 2001) can be seen as a descriptive definition suggesting that dyslexia is

> a combination of abilities and difficulties which affect the learning process in one or more of reading, spelling and writing. Accompanying weaknesses may be identified in areas of speed of processing, short-term memory, sequencing, auditory and/or visual perception, spoken language and motor skills. It is particularly related to mastering and using written language, which may include alphabetic, numeric and musical notation.

The Adult Dyslexia Organisation definition is also a descriptive one, but highlights the individuality of dyslexic people:

> Dyslexia may be caused by a combination of phonological, visual and auditory processing deficits. Word retrieval and speed of processing difficulties may also be present. A number of possible underlying biological causes of these cognitive deficits have been identified and it is probable that in any one individual there may be several causes. While the dyslexic individual may experience difficulties in the acquisition of reading, writing and spelling, they can be taught strategies and alternative learning methods to overcome most of these and other difficulties. Every dyslexic person is different and should be treated as an individual. Many show talents actively sought by employers, and the same factors that cause literacy difficulties may also be responsible for

highlighting positive attributes – such as problem-solving which can tap resources which lead to more originality and creativity. (Schloss, in Reid and Kirk 2001)

These definitions support the view that dyslexia relates to a broad range of difficulties associated with literacy and learning, that individual differences will be present, that some students with dyslexia can have positive attributes and that any difficulties are only part of the overall picture.

Discrepancy definitions, based on the unexpected discrepancy between ability and performance, have also been used widely, but this has been criticised by some researchers because of the lack of qualitative differences in reading errors between children from high and low IQ groups. However, it can be used by some education authorities in relation to allocating resources and determining cut-off points for provision (Pumfrey 1996). But as Pumfrey points out, 'establishing a resource allocation model that is explicit, open, fair and theoretically defensible requires considerable professional knowledge...making the model accord with the law requires additional sensitivity' (p. 20). The controversies and uncertainties regarding definitions and the responses to definitions in terms of identification, assessment and support motivated the British Psychological Society to convene a working party on this issue. The subsequent working party report 'Dyslexia, Literacy and Psychological Assessment' (BPS 1999) opted for a working definition of dyslexia because the working party felt that a working definition did not require any causal explanation. The working definition they opted for was as follows: 'Dyslexia is evident when accurate and fluent word reading and/or spelling develops very incompletely or with great difficulty' (p. 18). This definition should, however, be seen within the context of the report which is based on the well-established Frith and Morton causal modelling framework (Frith 2002) and provides a theoretical framework for educational psychologists in relation to assessment of dyslexia. The authors accept that it requires to be operationalised for different educational contexts.

An example of an operational definition can be seen in the East Renfrewshire Education Authority policy documentation on dyslexia. The definition used by this education authority is similar to that provided by the BDA (Peer 2001) but develops it by using operational criteria based on identification in the early stages; assessment, including a stepped process of identification and assessment; and the range of support in terms of strategies and provision (East Renfrewshire Council 1999).

The situation where a variety of definitions of essentially the same condition are in current use begs a crucial question – Why? The answer to this lies in the recent research activities in the field of dyslexia; the historical context of dyslexia; and the purpose for which one, or an organisation or authority, requires a definition.

Nicolson (2001) suggests that the advantage of the label 'dyslexia' is 'that it has no intrinsic meaning. It does not in itself provide information on causes, or whether it describes visual, phonological, motor, or any combination' (p. 5). Dyslexia therefore does not necessarily imply a unitary set of characteristics, but rather a syndrome or condition which requires specialised assessment and teaching in order to identify both the specific cluster of strengths and difficulties and to identify appropriate learning and teaching strategies.

In relation to research in the neurosciences, genetic studies have sought to highlight the interactive role of clusters of genes that contribute to the difficulties associated with dyslexia, which indicates that there is likely to be more than one cause of dyslexia. A range of contributory factors, such as biological, cognitive and environmental factors, have been attributed to dyslexia. For this reason it is important to have a wide-ranging working definition of dyslexia that can be operationalised for one's specific teaching and educational context.

Historically, definitions have been used to label rather than inform, and certainly it has been necessary for dyslexic children to acquire the label 'dyslexia' as a prerequisite to specialised support, and this situation still prevails in relation to support for examinations. A definition, however, should be more than a label or even an extended label. It is interesting that the BPS, in the working party report, opted for a working definition of dyslexia. Whether one agrees or not with the actual working definition used in the report is irrelevant; the important point is that service providers, speech therapists, psychologists, education authorities and course organisers may each have the need for their own working definition which they can operationalise to fit into their own working practices. A definition should be informative and not merely an extended label.

In the Republic of Ireland, a Government Task Force on Dyslexia (2001) proposed a definition that refers to a range of factors that may be implicated in dyslexia. The definition, which reflects a return to using the term 'dyslexia' instead of 'specific learning disability', is as follows:

> Dyslexia is manifested in a continuum of specific learning difficulties related to the acquisition of basic skills in reading, spelling, and/or writing, such difficulties being unexpected in relation to an individual's other abilities and educational experiences. Dyslexia can be described at the neurological, cognitive and behavioural levels. It is typically characterised by inefficient information processing, including difficulties in phonological processing, working memory, rapid naming and automaticity of basic skills. Difficulties in organisation, sequencing, and motor skills may also be present. (Task Force on Dyslexia 2001: 28)

As an addendum to this definition, the Task Force noted that learning difficulties arising from dyslexia

- occur across the lifespan, and may manifest themselves in different ways at different ages;
- may co-exist with difficulties in the area of number;
- may be associated with early spoken language difficulties;
- may be alleviated by appropriate intervention;
- increase or reduce in severity depending on environmental factors;
- occur in all socio-economic circumstances;
- co-exist with other learning difficulties such as Attention Deficit Disorder, and may or may not represent a primary difficulty.

Definitions: key aspects

If we were to identify key aspects to be included in a working/ operational definition of dyslexia we would suggest the following:

- recognition of a different **processing style** which can highlight **good problem-solving skills** and a degree of creativity;
- **possibly disadvantaged in left hemisphere processing** with resultant **difficulties in phonological processing**;
- **discrepancies in performances** in different areas of the curriculum;
- descriptive general **observable behaviours** associated with dyslexia, including strengths; and
- **practical implications for specific contexts** – classroom, training course, assessment, workplace, careers advisers, employers.

Definitions are important – they can guide identification, support, and policy and practice. It is important that they incorporate evidence from a range of research including the neurosciences, and also that they provide some observable criteria, which can assist in identification and support. Equally, it is also important that a definition does not become a generic label open to misinterpretation and abuse. It is therefore important to recognise that a definition of dyslexia should be contextualised for a purpose and context to make it meaningful for a specific educational or work context. Definitions need to inform and the concept of a working definition should do exactly that.

Some scientific research

There is little doubt that research in dyslexia and its impact on practice has increased in recent years. There has been considerable activity, for example, in the area of phonological awareness, and this is reflected in the development of assessment and teaching materials such as the Phonological Abilities Test (Muter, Hulme and Snowling 1997), the Phonological Assessment Battery (Fredrickson et al. 1997) and many phonological teaching approaches such as Sound Linkage (Hatcher 1994) and the Phonological Awareness Training Programme (Wilson 1993). This particular area of research is highlighted because of its direct impact on teaching and classroom practices.

Four overlapping dimensions can be identified in relation to one's understanding of dyslexia. These are: neurological/physiological; psychological/cognitive; educational/classroom dimensions; and environmental factors. This division illustrates the breadth of the current research activity and the interactive nature of dyslexia. Due to this wide range of factors there are also wide-ranging professional perspectives noted in the dyslexia research from the fields of education; psychology; speech and language therapy; occupational and movement therapy; and other clinical and health professions.

Neurological/physiological

The work of Galaburda (1993) has had a significant impact in both the conceptualisation of dyslexia and in practice. Essentially Galaburda suggests that the processing patterns of dyslexic people in the left and right hemispheres show differences in relation to non-dyslexic people. The implication of this is that those with a dyslexic profile can have right hemisphere preference for learning that can place them at a disadvantage in left hemisphere tasks, such as reading accuracy. Right hemisphere processing relates to tasks that require a 'global' holistic approach while left hemisphere processing involves analysis of detail and small chunks of information.

West (1997) has utilised Galaburda's research to show that dyslexic people who are right hemisphere processors can actually be at an advantage in some situations such as learning tasks which require some creativity and random thinking, and indeed in some subjects such as art and music. This emphasises the positive side of dyslexia.

Bakker *et al* (1994) in the 'balance model' which has been replicated in different countries (Robertson 1997; Bakker and Robertson 2002), identifies different types of readers, 'perceptual' and 'linguistic', each with a different hemispheric preference and each having implications for teaching. Bakker and Robertson (2002) have shown some hereditary trends in their research, and the work of Pennington and colleagues in Colorado, and Stein in the UK has done much to advance the knowledge base relating to genetic aspects of dyslexia.

There is also evidence of visual factors relating to dyslexia (Everatt 2002). Eden *et al.* (1996) show how dyslexic people can have abnormalities associated with the magnocellular sub-system which relates to visual processing, the work of Stein (1995) revealed convergence difficulties causing binocular instability, and Wilkins (1995) has shown how some dyslexic children may benefit from, for example, coloured overlays due to difficulties in some visual processes. Stein (2002) has shown how the magnocellular system can relate to other factors associated with dyslexia such as the role of the cerebellum and phonological processing. The role of deficits in essential fatty acids has been supported by the work of Richardson which has implications for dietary factors associated with dyslexia and learning.

Fawcett, Nicholson and Dean (1996) have shown how cerebellar impairment may be implicated with dyslexia and may be linked to difficulties in phonological processing as well as balance. These factors are represented in the Dyslexia Screening Test (Fawcett and Nicolson 1997).

Cognitive

In general terms dyslexia can be viewed as a difficulty with phonological processing. Hagtvet (1997), in a Norwegian study, showed that a phonological deficit at age six was the strongest predictor of reading difficulties. Other studies highlighted in Hulme and Snowling (1997) have shown speech rate to be a strong predictor of dyslexic difficulties, and this is reflected in the development of the Phonological Abilities Test (Muter, Hulme and Snowling 1997) and the Phonological Assessment Battery (Frederickson *et al.* 1997). The phonological

representations model as a core difficulty in dyslexi
by Snowling (2000) who suggests that the phonolo
which affects one's reading accuracy and fluency is
IQ discrepancies. Discrepancies between listenin
comprehension, and sight and regular spelling have bee
Weedon and Reid (2001) in the development of a group screening ior
profiling literacy difficulties – the Listening and Literacy Index.

Wolf (1991, 1996; Wolf and O'Brien 2001) highlights the 'double
deficit hypothesis', indicating that dyslexic children can have
difficulties with both phonological processing and naming speed. It is
not surprising, therefore, that speed of processing and semantic
fluency are included in some tests for dyslexic children. Badian (1997)
provides evidence for a triple deficit hypotheses, implying that ortho-
graphic factors involving visual skills should also be considered.

The role of metacognition in learning is of great importance as this
relates to the learners' awareness of thinking and learning. Tunmer
and Chapman (1996) have shown how dyslexic children have poor
metacognitive awareness and this leads them to adopt inappropriate
learning behaviours in reading and spelling. Similarly, difficulties in
automaticity (Fawcett and Nicolson 1992) implies that dyslexic
learners may not readily consolidate new learning, and therefore may
find it difficult to change inappropriate learning habits, requiring
additional time to achieve automaticity in a particular skill. Other
processing difficulties have also been linked to dyslexia, such as
auditory processing (Johanson 1997) from which a programme of
sound therapy has been developed. Some related motor integration
programmes have also been developed to help enhance the learning
skills of dyslexic children (Dobie 1998; McPhillips *et al* 2000).

Education/classroom dimensions

It is encouraging that research is impacting on practice. Education
authorities' policies on dyslexia, staff development, classroom-based
assessment, computer programmes and curriculum materials
focusing on differentiation all facilitate access to the full curriculum
for dyslexic children. Early identification and early intervention are
seen as priority areas and recent research and materials help to
support this. There is also an increased interest in bilingual dyslexic
learners and, as indicated in the previous chapter, there is a
significant need to develop culture-fair assessment in this area.
Research, therefore, in dyslexia can be viewed from neurological,

itive and classroom dimensions, and together these provide a
und basis for staff development and assessment, teaching, and
classroom practices which enhance the opportunities for success for
all dyslexic children from early years to higher education.

Environmental factors

As indicated above, dyslexia can be seen more readily in certain
contexts. It is not surprising, therefore, that the learning environment
can be an influential factor. It is important that classroom factors are
considered in order to make the learning situation dyslexia-friendly.
Often dyslexic children are quite sensitive and quite vulnerable to the
learning environment and their performances can vary depending on
their level of ease with the classroom climate and general learning
environment. It is also important to consider that visual stimuli may be
more meaningful to them than words. Therefore a visual-orientated
environment can be considered dyslexia-friendly. The learning
environment mediates across all the three factors mentioned earlier –
the biological; the cognitive; and the educational. It can be suggested
the environment includes aspects such as 'learning opportunities' as
well as school and education authority policy on dyslexia.

Policy and provision

Policy, therefore, is important in ensuring that the learning
environment is accessible and effective for dyslexic learners. A
considerable number of education authorities have developed policies
on dyslexia, and disability legislation (Disability Discrimination Act
1995) which originally applied to the workplace now applies to
education.

Teachers feel more secure in dealing with dyslexia if they know the
education authority has a policy that can be applied readily and
understood by both teachers and parents. There are many examples of
authority-wide initiatives in policy. The dyslexia-friendly schools
campaign described in the previous chapter has resulted in a number
of policy documents being produced in England and Wales, such as
that in Swansea. In Scotland policies in East Renfrewshire, Fife and
Edinburgh, and many other areas are based on early identification and
intervention. These programmes focus on literacy support for all
children and early identification and assessment of those pupils with
specific difficulties in literacy. Some of the aspects included in

policies and programmes are the design and promotion of a literacy-rich environment in school and the wider community, effective assessment of the difficulties and the development of links between school and community. Although these policies emphasise early intervention and the early years, the overall aim is to make literacy accessible and to promote the wider use of literacy in school and community settings in a positive and dyslexia-aware manner.

In the City of Edinburgh, much of the policy has been developed into support packages and staff and parent development initiatives. For example, the in-service training pack on specific learning difficulties contains sections on specific difficulties in subject classes, the development of appropriate curriculum materials for pupils with dyslexia and practical advice on meeting individual needs. A more recent support pack for preschool and primary teachers contains a comprehensive guide for the class teacher looking at many of the aspects contained in this book, including indicators of dyslexia and strategies for dealing with reading, writing and spelling difficulties, as well as information on learning styles.

It is important that such guidance, contextualised for each education authority, is available to provide teachers with both the knowledge and the security which assist them to deal successfully with dyslexic children. It is important that the development of policies should be collaborative. A good example of this is the policy document called 'Specific Learning Difficulties: Professionals, Parents and Pupils' (Fife Education Authority 1996). Such collaboration is necessary to obtain the perspectives of all parties involved in dyslexia, and the views of parents are particularly useful.

Similarly, the notion of 'dyslexia-friendly schools' (Mackay 2001) focuses on a culture or ethos of dyslexia-friendly methodology and materials, which include empowerment, which recognises the learning preferences of dyslexic children and provides 'safe' opportunities for them to utilise these preferences; good practice which 'open doors rather than close them'; and a supportive environment. Essentially, a dyslexia-friendly school should empower the learner to operate at an ability-appropriate level. Too often dyslexic children and young people do not fulfil their potential at school because their abilities go unnoticed and, consequently, they underachieve. It is important, therefore, that awareness of dyslexia should be transformed into policy and that this should result in effective and positive practice.

Chapter 3

Identification and Assessment

The class teacher has an important role to play in the process of assessment. In fact the class teacher is the one who is in the best position to identify dyslexia initially and enlist others to assist in the assessment and support process. The class teacher and the subject teacher work with the child more than others and would be able to highlight any discrepancies or unexpected performances. This is particularly the case with the discrepancy between oral and written performances. This chapter will outline the main aspects the class teacher should look out for and how teachers can do this within the curriculum and their own subject areas.

The difficulties

The difficulties the class teacher can identify include the following characteristics:

- reading – hesitates over words; misses out words; makes semantic errors such as reading the word 'bus' for 'car'; misses off word endings; omission or confusion of small words such as 'for' and 'of'; difficulty with polysyllabic words such as 'preliminary' (they may say 'preminary' or 'premilinary'); confusing letters with similar shapes such as 'm' and 'w' and 'u' and 'n'; confusing whole words which are visually similar such as 'was' and 'saw'; lack of consistency in the use of tense; grammatical difficulties.

- spelling – may spell phonetically, e.g. 'elefant' for 'elephant'; omit parts of the word (middle or end); difficulties with 'er'/'or'/'ar' endings; inconsistencies in spelling particular words; difficulty in spelling commonly used words as well as irregular words; unusual spellings may be described as bizarre; difficulty with some sounds such as 's' and 'z'; letters or syllables out of sequence.
- memory – difficulty remembering instructions; difficulty remembering numbers in sequence; difficulty remembering something if doing something else at the same time or distracted; difficulty remembering facts and dates; may have difficulty in remembering appointments; needs cues to remember things; may use unusual memory aids to help remember appointments/dates.
- writing – may have difficulty in copying from the board; inconsistent handwriting style; reluctance to write.
- organisation – difficulty in organising homework and workload; poor organisation of work in notebook; notes may be disorganised; may have difficulty in organising new facts and relating these to previous learning.
- sequencing – difficulty in putting information in the correct order; difficulty in sequencing letters, words and numbers; may have difficulty sequencing days of week/months of year.
- difficulty following instructions – difficulty with more than one instruction; difficulty carrying out instructions in the correct sequence.

In addition to these difficulties the child with dyslexia may also display discrepancies in different areas of the curriculum. For example, they may be competent in Art but have difficulty with English, although some dyslexic students can show some abilities in English Literature, although their reading may still be at a slower pace.

Other discrepancies can include that between oral and written performance and quite often there is a discrepancy between ability and actual performance.

It is important, therefore, for the class teacher to have some knowledge of the characteristics of dyslexia and specific examples of the difficulties displayed by dyslexic children. It is also worth remembering that not all dyslexic children will display all of these characteristics – each is an individual, although they have some common dyslexic difficulties, and this needs to be acknowledged in both the assessment and the teaching. Individual differences can be identified through learning styles and learning strategies and this will be discussed later in this book.

It is useful, however, for the class teacher to have some form of observation framework to use in the classroom situation to gather information which can help to inform an assessment and provide some pointers for appropriate teaching.

Observation assessment

Observation assessment can provide important information on the learner's strengths and weaknesses and provide some pointers for teaching strategies.

An observation schedule or framework can be constructed but it is important that it is flexible and adaptable to different learning situations.

Throughout the observation it is important to record not only what the student does or can do but *how* the response is achieved – the cues required, and the level and extent of the assistance needed at the stages the student needs to go through to solve a problem or obtain a response.

With increased importance being placed on metacognitive aspects of learning – that is how children learn – activities such as observation can have an important role to play in finding out how the child learns and the strengths and difficulties experienced in the learning task.

A framework for observation

The framework below highlights a broad range of areas that can relate to some of the difficulties experienced by children with dyslexia. It is important to gather information that relates to the child, the learning situation and the context. The aim is not just to find out how or why the child is having difficulty, but also to gain some insight and understanding into the strategies and processes of learning for that learner.

A framework for observational assessment for dyslexia can therefore include the areas listed below but can be contextualised for each subject area of the curriculum. This is important as the performances of dyslexic children can fluctuate quite considerably in different subject areas.

Attention
- length of attention span;
- conditions when attention is enhanced;

- factors contributing to distractability;
- attention/distractability under different learning conditions.

Organisation
- organisational preferences;
- degree of structure required;
- organisation of work, desk, self;
- reactions to imposed organisation.

Sequencing
- able to follow sequence of instructions – type of help required to enable instructions to be followed;
- general difficulty with sequencing: work; carrying out instructions; words when reading; individual letters in written work;
- difficulty sequencing pictures or diagrams.

Interaction
- degree of interaction with peers, adults;
- preferred interaction – one-to-one; small groups; whole class;
- how interaction is sustained – needs to talk or be involved in activities to sustain attention.

Language
- expressive language;
- is meaning accurately conveyed?
- spontaneous/prompted;
- is there appropriate use of natural breaks in speech?
- expressive language in different contexts, e.g. one-to-one, small group, class group;
- errors, omissions and difficulties in conversation and responses, e.g. mispronunciations, questions to be repeated or clarified.

Comprehension
- How does the child comprehend information?
- What type of cues most readily facilitate comprehension?
- Use of schema. Does the child have concepts or a working framework of the new learning?
- What type of instructions are most easily understood – written, oral, visual?
- How readily can knowledge be transferred to other areas?

Reading
- reading preferences – aloud, silent;
- type of errors:

Visual
- discrimination between letters which look the same;
- inability to appreciate that the same letter may look different, e.g. 'G' 'g';
- omitting or transposing part of a word (this could indicate a visual segmentation difficulty).

Auditory
- difficulties in auditory discrimination;
- inability to hear consonant sounds in initial, medial or final position;
- auditory sequencing;
- auditory blending;
- auditory segmentation.

Motivation/initiative
- interest level of child;
- How is motivation increased – What kind of prompting and cueing is necessary?
- To what extent does the child take responsibility for own learning?
- What kind of help is required?

Self-concept
- What tasks are more likely to be tackled with confidence?
- When is confidence low?
- self-concept and confidence in different contexts.

Relaxation
- Is the child relaxed when learning?
- evidence of tension and relaxation.

Learning preferences
These include the following learning preferences:

- auditory;
- visual;
- oral;
- kinesthetic;

- tactile;
- global;
- analytic.

It is important, therefore, to note in observational assessment the preferred mode of learning. Many children will of course show preferences and skills in a number of modes of learning. For that reason, multi-sensory teaching is recommended for dyslexic children in order to accommodate as many learning modalities as possible.

Learning context

When assessing the nature and degree of the difficulty experienced by the child, it is important to take into account the learning context. This context, depending on the learner's preferred style can either exacerbate the difficulty or minimise the problem. The contextual factors below should therefore be considered:

- classroom – how is the classroom organised (lighting, sound, activity in class) – is it organised for group work?
- role of teacher – type of teacher input (auditory); level of structure provided by the teacher;
- task – Is the task understood? Can the dyslexic child follow the sequence of the task? Will group work be more effective with the task?
- materials/resources – reading level of materials; range of resources; how much responsibility is given to the learner in selecting resources.

Observation to identify the full extent of the learner's strengths and weaknesses in different subject areas therefore needs to incorporate a holistic perspective. This can be done by:

- observing components within a framework for learning;
- observing some factors within that framework associated with specific dyslexia;
- observing preferred styles of learning;
- acknowledging the importance of the learning context.

Primary/secondary liaison

This is an extremely important aspect and can provide the secondary teacher with a picture of the child – information that can complement any observational data gathered in the classroom. Primary–secondary transfer is, by its very nature, a period which can affect pupils' self-esteem and general confidence (Reid 1986). Students with dyslexia can be extremely vulnerable at this point. It is, therefore, extremely important that early and effective liaison between primary and secondary schools takes place.

While it is accepted that there are some practical constraints in relation to this, timetabling and school policy should nevertheless recognise the need to allow key members of staff sufficient flexibility to allow for effective liaison. Such liaison should commence as early as possible during the school year prior to transfer. This would allow, for example, an opportunity for some key staff from the secondary school to monitor the progress of the dyslexic pupil throughout the final year at primary. This is clearly preferable to being handed a report – even if it is a comprehensive one – just before transfer takes place. Early liaison allows the secondary staff to build up a picture of the pupil; to begin to plan and prepare subject teachers in the secondary school to deal with the kinds of difficulties presented; and to report on the strategies used during in the primary class.

Metacognitive aspects in assessment

Metacognition essentially means thinking about thinking. This information can be obtained by observing and discussing the learning process with the child. This is important because, by examining how children learn, information can be gleaned to help in the development of materials for each subject area and strategies for teaching in different subjects. This can be vital to helping dyslexic children make reading and learning more meaningful and to help in the transfer of learning from one situation to another. Flavell (1979) greatly influenced the field of metacognition and its applications to the classroom. Since then many studies have been conducted in metacognition and various models have been developed. Brown *et al.* (1986) provides a model containing four main variables which are found in the learning situation. These include:

- **text** – the material to be learnt;
- **task** – the purpose of reading;
- **strategies** – how the learner understands and remembers information;
- **characteristics of the learner** – prior experience, background knowledge, interests, motivation.

In order to do this effectively, the class teacher would need to build up a good knowledge of each of the students with dyslexia. Only then would this type of individualisation of the curriculum be possible. Some of the most effective strategies for dyslexic children result from this type of curriculum differentiation made possible through knowledge of the learning characteristics of the student.

Tod and Fairman (2001) also put forward the view that metacognitive factors are important and have particular relevance to examinations. Very often students with dyslexia do not understand what examiners are actually looking for in a response to the question set in the exam. If they understand what the examiners want then dyslexic students can set appropriate targets for themselves. According to Tod and Fairman dyslexic students need to know that in 'three mark' questions, three clear sentences written on separate lines are more likely to get three marks than a rambling paragraph from which information has to be extracted. They suggest that when shown an 'exemplar' answer, most students can get closer to reproducing it. One of the key aspects of metacognition is that it involves being aware of the task and the processes involved in completing the task. Dyslexic students may find that difficult, but Tod and Fairman suggest that students could work together to reinforce what needs to be included and can remind each other to include what tends to be omitted. They feel that peer marking, handled responsibly, can be very useful in enabling students to mark objectively using marking schemes.

Multiple intelligences

Howard Gardner developed the concept of multiple intelligences. These can be utilised in the assessment and learning situation. Multiple intelligence, in fact, can be used as a guide to developing both teaching and assessment materials.

Multiple intelligences refer to eight different forms of intelligence (Lazear 1999). These are:

1. **Verbal/linguistic** – reading; vocabulary; creative writing; poetry; debate.

2. **Logical/mathematical** – abstract symbols; number sequences; calculation; problem-solving; pattern games.

3. **Visual/spatial** – imagery; imagination; colour schemes; patterns/designs; painting; drawing; mind mapping.

4. **Body/kinesthetic** – role play; physical gestures; drama; physical exercise; sports.

5. **Musical/rhythmic** – rythmic patterns; music; sounds; rythmic patterns.

6. **Interpersonal** – giving feedback; recognising other people's feelings; cooperative learning strategies; collaboration skills; group projects.

7. **Intrapersonal** – reflection; metacognition techniques; thinking strategies; emotional awareness; concentration skills.

8. **Naturalist** – this refers to ones familiarity with the environment, countryside and different species of wildlife, flora, birds and animals.

Much of the teaching in schools appears to focus a great deal on the verbal/linguistic area. Yet, as can be seen above, this is only one of eight possible forms of knowing and understanding. Below is an example of how the verbal/linguistic area can be made dyslexia-friendly through applying the multiple intelligences framework.

It is important to recognise the skills of each child and to use those skills to achieve success. For example, the dyslexic child may have difficulty in the verbal/linguistic areas but have skills in the interpersonal area. This area can be used to develop confidence and raise self-concept in the learning situation. For example, by nominating the child with good interpersonal skills as a leader in a group project, even though he/she may have difficulty in reading the instructions (others in the group can do this).

Lazear (1991; 1999) illustrates how to make verbal/lingustic activities user-friendly. This can provide a good model for teaching dyslexic children. For example, in history, games and debates can be helpful, as can creating limericks about historical characters and even compiling a notebook of historical jokes. In mathematics, making up puns using mathematic vocabulary or terms, or solving problems with a partner (one solves and the other explains the process), and writing a series of story problems for others to solve. Similarly, in

Table 3.1 Lesson Planning Ideas: Verbal/Linguistic

HISTORY	MATHEMATICS	LANGUAGE ARTS	SCIENCE & HEALTH	GLOBAL STUBIES & GEOGRAPHY	PRACTICAL ARTS & P.E.	FINE ARTS
Play 'What's My Line?' with figures from history	Write a series of story problems for others to solve	Teach 'concept mapping' to help remember content	Write a humorous story using science vocabulary/formulas	Read stories, myths, and poetry from other cultures	Give verbal explanation of gymnastic routines	Listen to a piece of music make up a story about it
Debate important issues and decisions from the past	Explain how to work a problem to others while they follow	Write a sequel/next episode to a story or play	Create a diary on 'The Life of a Red Blood Cell'	Hold a 'Countries of the World' spelling and pronunciation bee	Write instructions for use and care of shop machines	Verbally describe an object while a partner draws it
Create limericks about key historical events	Make up puns using math vocabulary or terms	Create cross-word puzzles/word jumbles for vocabulary words	Write steps used in an experiment so someone else can do it	Keep an 'Insights from other Cultures for Us' log	Tell another how to run a word processing program—then do it	Tell a partner the steps to a dance while they perform it
Study poetry from different periods of history	Solve problems with a partner—one solves and one explains process	Play 'New Word for the Day' game—learn it/use it during the day	Make up an imaginary conversation between parts of the body	Study a road map and give verbal instructions to get someplace	Pretend you're a radio sportscaster describing a game in process	Turn a Greek/Shakespearean tragedy into a situation comedy
Compile a notebook of history jokes	Create poems telling when to use different math operations	Practice impromptu speaking and writing	Give a speech on 'Ten steps to healthful living'	Learn basic conversation in several foreign languages	Play 'Recipe Jeopardy'—make questions for answers given	Describe an emotion/mood and play music it suggests

(reproduced with permission Lazear 1991)

science students can be encouraged to write steps in an experiment so that someone else can do it and make up an imaginary conversation between different parts of the body.

Materials for all subjects, in fact, can be adapted using multiple intelligences as a guide. Clearly, intelligences such as visual/spatial and kinesthetic can be used very effectively as these are the areas which are very likely the natural preferences for learning for dyslexic children.

For example, visual/spatial aspects in history can involve imaginary interviews with people from the past and visual flow charts, timelines and diagrams. A good example of this can be seen in the Heinemann history series 'Explore', by Richard Dargie. Each book in the series and the accompanying CD-ROM utilises timelines to help readers develop understanding of time and historical sequence, the use of sources which involve problem-solving skills and, generally, an emphasis on enquiry and investigation rather than passive information.

Although 'multiple intelligence' strategies seem to be directed at teaching strategies and the development of teaching materials, they can also be used as a guide for assessment. For example, portfolio assessment developed over time can help the dyslexic child display a fuller range of his/her abilities. Similarly, assessment which involves problem-solving rather than knowledge of facts can also be dyslexia-friendly. Although we are working within an established examination system which is mainly directed towards the verbal/linguistic area, the multiple intelligences framework can be used in teaching and in informal assessment. It is, of course, also important that some effort goes into preparing the dyslexic student for the traditional examination system.

Preparation for examinations

Examinations, and the examination system, do not naturally favour the dyslexic student. Factors such as writing within a time limit, reading under pressure and recalling information almost instantly are usually those which the dyslexic student finds difficult. The help which can be provided, such as a 'reader' to read the script, or a scribe, can be useful, but requires considerable preparation and practice. Such forms of aid should not be provided only at examination time. The student would need to become familiar with this form of help if it were to be seriously considered. This emphasises that preparation for the support needed for examinations should begin virtually as soon as the pupil enters secondary school.

It is important, therefore, that dyslexic students are known, not only to specialist teachers but to all subject teachers, since the type of examination help required will vary from subject to subject. Identifying students for examination provision and helping to maximise the benefits of these provisions should, therefore, be seen as a whole-school issue. Administrative structures, therefore, need to be in place to monitor these arrangements. This may include a school sub-group, preferably involving the school psychologist, guidance teacher, management, support and some subject teachers. The function of such a group would be to discuss students who may need special arrangements, and how these could be effectively implemented within the school system. It is important that dyslexic students are not unduly restricted because of the nature of the school examination system, and that all their abilities are assessed equally and not only their performances in the area of literacy.

Tod and Fairman (2001) suggest that dyslexic students need to understand subject-marking schemes. They believe that many students struggle to understand why they only get a D grade because they do not realise what they could have included to get more marks. In some courses markers may try to identify key words to identify if the student has covered the relevant points. It is important, therefore, that students need to know this, particularly as students with dyslexia often miss out on some of the key points because of time or other factors associated with reading speed. Tod and Fairman believe that when students are clear about the marking scheme they can be supported to produce a match between what is required and what is produced.

Screening tests

There are some standardised and commercially available screening tests which can be readily used in the secondary school context. These include the Dyslexia Screening test (Fawcett and Nicolson 1996), the Bangor Dyslexia Screening test (Miles 1983) and the Lucid Assessment System for Schools (Secondary) (LASS), ages 11–15 (Horne, Singleton and Thomas 1999) (Lucid Software), and Lucid Adults Dyslexia Screening (LADS), adult 16+ (Lucid Software). Additionally, a computer-aided diagnostic assessment and profiling kit with a CD-ROM, manual and photocopiable resources for specific learning difficulties, including dyslexia (Special Needs Assessment Portfolio (SNAP)) (Weedon and Reid 2003) is available for collaborative use by class teacher, specialist teacher, parents and other professionals who may be involved with the student.

Bangor Dyslexia Test

This is a commercially available short screening test developed from work conducted at Bangor University (Miles 1983). The test is now used in many different countries. It is divided into the following sections:

- left-right (body parts)
- repeating polysyllabic words
- subtraction
- tables
- months forward/reversed
- digits forward/reversed
- b–d confusion
- familial incidence.

It is important to note that this test is only intended as a screening device to find out whether the subject's difficulties are, or are not, typically dyslexic and may therefore offer a contribution towards an understanding of the subject's difficulties. It should not therefore be seen as a definitive diagnosis.

Dyslexia Screening Test (DST)

The authors of this test (Fawcett and Nicolson 1996) indicate that it was developed due to both the wider theoretical understanding of dyslexia, particularly since the publication of the earlier Bangor Dyslexia Test, and the changes in the British educational system, particularly relating to the formal procedures for assessing whether children have special educational needs. It may also have a use, according to the authors, of assessing whether some children should have extra time in examinations.

The Dyslexia Screening Test can be used for children between 6.6 to 16.5 years of age. There are also two others developed by the same authors for younger children, Dyslexia Early Screening Test (Nicolson and Fawcett 1998) and The Pre-School Screening Test

(PREST) (Fawcett, Nicolson and Lee 2001). The PREST can screen children aged 3 years 6 months, to 4 years 5 months. There is also an adult version – Dyslexia Adult Screening Test (Fawcett and Nicolson 1998). The test consists of the following attainment tests:

- one minute reading
- two minute spelling
- one minute writing

and the following diagnostic tests:

- rapid naming
- bead threading
- postural stability
- phonemic segmentation
- backwards digit span
- nonsense passage reading
- verbal and semantic fluency.

LASS – Lucid Assessment System for Schools (Secondary) (Horne, Singleton and Thomas 1999)

The Lucid/CoPS range of tests benefit from the advantages associated with computer programs such as greater provision in presenting assessment tasks and greater accuracy in measuring responses. The programme can be administered with only the minimum of training and generally provides a greater degree of objectivity than some other forms of screening. These school-based tests have the potential therefore to fulfil an important function, particularly in curriculum planning for children with dyslexia difficulties.

Lucid Adult Dyslexia Screening (LADS) (Singleton 2002)

The Lucid Adult Dyslexia Screening is a computerised test designed to screen for dyslexia in persons of 16 years and older. It comprises four assessment modules: word recognition; word constructions; word memory; and reasoning. It is suggested that the first three are dyslexia-sensitive measures. Each of the four modules takes around five minutes to complete and the tests are self-administered.

LADS is designed to be used for routine screening for dyslexia and individual screening in adults and can be used in universities and colleges as well as prison and youth offender units and employment centres. The LADS provides a categorisation of persons taking the test into 'low probability of dyslexia', 'borderline', 'moderate probability' and 'high probability'. The report provides a brief description of the results and this method can provide a cost-effective initial screening for dyslexia.

Special Needs Assessment Profile

The Special Needs Assessment Profile (SNAP) is a computer-aided diagnostic assessment and profiling package that makes it possible to 'map' each student's own mix of problems onto an overall matrix of learning, behavioural and other difficulties. From this, clusters and patterns of weaknesses and strengths help to identify the core features of a student's difficulties – visual, dyslexic, dyspraxic, phonological, attentional or any other of the 15 key deficits targeted – and suggests a diagnosis that points the way forward for that individual student. It provides a structured profile which yields an overview at the early stages of 'School Action' in the Code of Practice, and also informs the process of external referral at 'School Action Plus'.

SNAP involves four steps:

Step 1 (*Pupil Assessment Pack*): structured questionnaire checklists for completion by class teachers and parents give an initial 'outline map' of the child's difficulties.

Step 2 (*CD-ROM*): the SENCO or Learning Support staff chart the child's difficulties, using the CD-ROM to identify patterns and target any further diagnostic follow-up assessments to be carried out at Step 3.

Step 3 (*User's Kit*): focused assessments from a photocopiable resource bank of quick diagnostic 'probes' yield a detailed and textured understanding of the child's difficulties.

Step 4 (*CD-ROM*): the computer-generated profile yields specific guidance on support (including personalised information sheets for parents) and practical follow-up.

The kit helps to facilitate the collaboration between different groups of professionals and between professionals and parents, which is vital in order to obtain a full picture of the students abilities and difficulties.

Role of other professionals

The class teacher has an important role to play in preparing the dyslexic student for examinations. The responsibility for this, however, is a shared one – it is a whole-school responsibility, and other professionals, specialist teachers and educational psychologists should be in a position to liaise with the subject teacher to ensure that the students needs can be adequately met.

Comments

Assessment, therefore, is not a one-off diagnostic exercise; it is a continuous and dynamic process that incorporates more than administering a test. The process is essentially a whole-school one, and assessment is therefore a whole-school responsibility. It is for that reason that policy and guidelines for school staff are essential. At the same time the class teacher is in a prime position to observe the progress and the difficulties experienced by students with dyslexia, and can be the first line in the identification and assessment. Above all, assessment should link to teaching and should provide the class/subject teacher with guidance in the development of teaching and curriculum materials. It has been expressed here that the effects of dyslexia can vary according to the learning situation, the task, the subject area and the curriculum. It is crucial, therefore, that the class teacher has the knowledge and the support to accommodate to the needs of students with dyslexia within the framework of the curriculum, and the different subject areas of the curriculum. Assessment and diagnosis should not be seen as the end of the process, but the beginning. It is ongoing, and the continuous monitoring of the progress of the student with dyslexia is as important as the initial diagnosis.

Chapter 4

Teaching and Learning

Linking assessment and teaching

It has been suggested that there is little point in assessing a child unless the assessment is accompanied by suggestions for teaching and provision. Other than knowing that there is a genuine reason for an individual's problems – which doesn't involve laziness or brain damage – there is perhaps some truth to this comment. However, there are many ways in which assessment can be carried out. Fundamentally, however, we must ensure that children receive the ongoing monitoring that they need to ensure that provision is effective and is altered when necessary.

Reid and Wearmouth (2002) describe the difference between *formative* and *summative* assessment and the links into teaching and learning.

Formative assessment is carried out by teachers to collect information and evidence about a pupil's literacy development and to plan the next step in his/her learning. It combines the assessment of skills required for specific tasks and pupil-referenced techniques where the same pupil's progress is tracked across time.

Summative assessment takes place at certain intervals when achievement has to be recorded and is intended to provide a global picture of the learner's literacy development to date. It requires a high degree of reliability, and may involve a combination of different types of assessment; for example, the measurement of individual pupil progression in learning against the criteria set, for example, in public examinations.

There are different types of assessment that can be used to assess a child's strengths and weaknesses as well as indicating where the child is at any place in time in specific areas of literacy and numeracy. In some cases it will be important to bring in the services and expertise of outside agencies, such as speech and language or occupational therapists. In some cases where self-esteem is on the downward spiral, there may be a need for an investigation into personality issues also. It is equally vital that parents and the child are brought into discussions and they, too, are encouraged to take responsibility for their part in the learning process. Educators must recognise that needs will change with the age and stage of learning. Any education plan must reflect this ongoing change and make adjustment for need as required.

We often hear that if a child has made progress over, for example, six months, in spelling and reading, he/she no longer needs help. Even if there were to be nine months' progress in a six-month period, there would be a need to ask more questions. Is the progress transferring across the curriculum? What happens when the child is asked to work under pressure? Until the child can function at both age-appropriate and intellectually appropriate levels, support must continue to be given. The level and type of support will, of course, change with need over time.

Curriculum factors

Dyslexic learners may try to conceal their difficulties when they see others around them succeeding and they are not. In many cases they may be well aware that others are less knowledgeable, but because they can write better they will achieve better marks. This can be very disheartening.

There are many ways to conceal failure. Montgomery (1998) cites withdrawal, avoidance, evasion, distraction, digression, disruption, clowning, daydreaming, negativism, absenteeism and cheating. Clowning is a common response of able pupils. As a result, it is clear that teachers have to offer their dyslexic children who need it a differentiated curriculum. This is one that both addresses the average to high intellectual potential, and, equally, addresses lower-level literacy (and possibly numeracy) abilities. If the range of specific learning difficulties, including dyslexia, is not addressed early on, there will be a worsening effect as the years progress. It is highly recommended that all children are screened for dyslexic-type difficulties so that an early intervention programme can be put in place. This is of greatest benefit to the individual, and can be financially very cost-effective. Multi-sensory teaching programmes alongside the development of those skills that are weak will ensure that, for the vast majority, success is the outcome. For younger learners, the use of cursive handwriting from the start is of great benefit to those who experience difficulties in the writing process.

Metacognitive awareness is of great value to all learners, particularly those who are dyslexic. Asking the 'why', 'purpose' and 'how' of oneself in relation to task fulfilment is key to an analytical mind. It is of particular value when learners have weak memories and often need to find alternative ways of retrieving information for academic success. Such programmes of learning should be part of school policy as should, for example, marking schemes which recognise the difference between knowledge and the way in which it is presented.

It must also be accepted that some dyslexic learners will be strong in some subjects, yet weaker in others. Typically, the acquisition of a modern foreign language may be quite problematic for some. In that case they should have the opportunity to learn in differing ways in various subject areas that are appropriate for them. This will allow them to learn through their strengths while developing their weaknesses.

The learner

The following comment by Brooks highlights the need to consider the emotional aspects of learning. There is much evidence to suggest that self-concept is one of the most influential predictors of success in learning. Brooks puts forward the following view:

> I have had the opportunity to work with many children and adolescents with learning disorders during the past thirty years. In conducting therapy with these youths, I became increasingly aware that most were burdened by feelings of low self-worth and incompetence and that many believed that their situation would not improve. Not surprisingly, this sense of hopelessness served as a major obstacle to future success. Once children believe that things will not improve, they are likely to engage in self-defeating ways of coping such as quitting or avoiding tasks, blaming others for their difficulties, or becoming class clowns or bullies. Thus, a negative cycle is often set in motion, intensifying feelings of defeat and despair. (Robert B. Brooks, PhD, Harvard Medical School, Cambridge, MA)

In order to prevent this demise into low self-esteem, with its accompanying negative consequences, there is a need to identify and intervene as early as possible. Appropriate provision should ensure that such learners go on to become successful adults. Many people consider those who are dyslexic to have a problem which is solely about reading. We know that this is absolutely not the case. Some people do have such a weakness, yet others do not. All seem to have a problem, however, with part of the writing process. Yet academic weaknesses are only a part of the story. It is of great concern that many dyslexic people do indeed experience that which Brooks outlined above. It is up to educators and parents to ensure that this does not happen.

The social-emotional needs of a learner are as important as the academic needs. In fact, it is true to say that if those other needs are not met, there will be a serious obstacle to the general opportunities for success. If you believe you cannot do it, you will not! Knowing how to present knowledge and information to the students in our classes will greatly determine absorption and understanding. If we are predominantly auditory learners ourselves, and only teach in the way we learn best, those in our classes who may prefer to acquire information in a visual way will find themselves at a great disadvantage. Goleman (1995) speaks of the need for empathy. This is highly relevant for these learners. There are those who prefer to ignore dyslexia altogether or, at the other extreme, be over sympathetic. Neither of these responses is appropriate. Understanding, together with structure, support and encouragement, are most useful for the success of the dyslexic learner. All learners have areas of strength – including those who appear to experience difficulty with the commitment of information onto paper. Many dyslexic people are highly creative in the visual arts, others in computing, yet others orally. Self-esteem always improves once strengths are identified and encouraged to flourish. Others in the class should be encouraged to go to that person for help in areas they find easy, if at all possible. In such a way, a good two-way buddy system works exceptionally well. Children need to have goals that they feel they can achieve. Small steps that are explicit and measurable are most effective, both academically and emotionally.

Some dyslexic learners will do well in a 'dyslexia-friendly' school. This will be most appropriate for those with mild-moderate difficulties. However, those with more severe need will undoubtedly need more intensive specialist help. All teachers need to take responsibility for children in their care across the school, subject teachers reinforcing the work of the specialist. In such a way dyslexic learners are most likely to fulfil their potential and ensure that they reach their individual targets – and the school will reach its goals.

Examinations

Coursework

The current examination system demands that students often have to produce a combination of coursework and written examinations. In order to produce good coursework, which carries much weight in many circumstances, it is essential to ensure that the student is well prepared and understands that which is being demanded of him. He will need the steps that are to be taken to be explained clearly; this may mean that they are repeated several times. Sometimes the thought of having to produce a major piece of written work alone can be quite overwhelming. Dyslexic students have been known to write pages of irrelevant material; guidelines are extremely useful. Monitoring is also important as it can prevent the student with dyslexia from going in completely the wrong direction in answering a question. It is sometimes a good idea to provide structure words – the key words that the student will very likely need to use. This prevents the wasting of valuable time while the student tries to think of these words. Students with dyslexia often have a word-finding difficulty and may not be able to access the correct word at the right time. Providing structure words, therefore, can help with this.

For example, if the student has to write a story on the Vikings, the following words could be provided as they will help the student with dyslexia to concentrate on the expressive writing process instead of attempting to retrieve words from memory:

Northmen Norse longship Knorrs sagas feasting monk Iona
Norway Sweden Denmark Baltic Sea Picts warriors galleys

Drafting

Drafting is an important aspect of students' work and particularly important for students with dyslexia. The processes involved in drafting work can be taught to all students quite comfortably within the framework of the classroom. This will help overcome the sense that there is too much to remember in one go. For example, the piece of written work can be drafted in stages – it is sometimes useful to also provide the student with a framework and structure, and this is almost essential for students with dyslexia. This framework can be in the form of the contents of the different stages, such as the introduction, main part and conclusion. For example, in the introduction the student may be encouraged to reflect on the actual question and task. What exactly is the question asking; what are the key points; why *are* these key points; where did you get this information from and how does this actually answer the question? These questions may seem fundamental, but often they have to be provided for the student with dyslexia – they can form a structure which can guide both the thinking and the writing process. It is also important to encourage the identifying of the main points – perhaps four or five main points that can be highlighted in the introduction. These can form the basis of the discussion in the main part of the essay and can help to provide a structure throughout the essay for the student with dyslexia. Techniques that take students with dyslexia through the stages of structure and planning, organisation and sequencing, comparing and contrasting, creative writing, punctuation, grammar and spelling will help them achieve their targets and keep them on track. They must be encouraged to refer back to the question from time to time to ensure that they are still on task.

Assuming they know how to use a library without support, create a bibliography or use an encyclopaedia or dictionary is unwise. They may be too embarrassed to tell you that they are experiencing difficulties and, therefore, they may need have this discussion with you in private.

If the coursework has a practical component, such as laboratory work, ensure that the student understands the safety regulations. Furthermore, as implied above, it is important to ensure they that have read and understood the assignment – they could be asked to explain it to you before commencement of the work. In a practical science piece of work, check that that they know where and how to enter their results in an organised and systematic fashion.

Revision

Revision is an important part of the preparation for examinations and it is important to ensure that revision time is built into the timetable. Dyslexic students may well experience considerable difficulty in committing large amounts of information from a range of subjects to memory at any one time. As they see their peers working and reciting vast tracts, this may well add to their sense of significant unease and possible failure. Therefore they should be taught not to rote learn but to understand the information and know how to apply their knowledge. These are essentially study skills and an important part of the teaching process to help dyslexic students.

They should be taught a range of study skill techniques that include: learning styles, thinking skills and Mind Mapping© strategies. They must be given a framework for study and a programme set up to ensure that it is adhered to in terms of preparation time and subject matter.

If the learner prefers learning in a group situation, for example, each person could be encouraged to take responsibility for one particular aspect of learning and for explaining it to the others. Other learners may prefer to use visual aids such as brightly coloured markers. Yet others may prefer to make up tunes and learn using rhythm. None is better than the other; what matters is that the learners are encouraged to find their best way of learning and to adapt their revision programme in that way.

Time is a really big issue for dyslexic students. They may feel totally overwhelmed at the number of subjects and the amount of information they have to absorb. A revision timetable for home and school is therefore critical.

Short breaks should be encouraged in the revision schedule – perhaps 40 minutes of study and ten minutes' break. This will ensure that the student is more able to concentrate and less likely to daydream.

Finally, if learners are given some past examination papers to use in a timed way at home, this will get them used to time limits and organisation of written responses.

The examination

Dyslexic learners are allowed specific provisions according to their individual needs. This is intended to give a fair balance for people who have difficulty in processing information in the same way as their peers, due to a disability. Dyslexia is one such disability. This may be anything from extra time to the use of a word-processor or a range of other possibilities. Schools and parents should liaise with the examination boards and ensure that the appropriate provision is made for each individual student. This should be sufficiently early to allow the student to be working in this way regularly, well before examinations are taken.

Before the commencement of the examination, staff need to ensure that their dyslexic students have remembered the relevant equipment for the particular examination. Include in this list a watch to ensure that they can more easily keep to time.

Remind them to take their time in reading the questions so that they are very clear what it is they are answering, and to then take a few minutes to organise their answers. Students need to be reminded to 'attack' the questions and prepare answers using well-rehearsed methods, e.g. Mind Maps© or spidergrams. Remind them to answer questions concisely and not to wander.

Finally, encourage them to read over their answers if they have time, ensuring that they have answered the correct questions and they have, as far as possible, self-corrected spelling, punctuation and grammar.

Relaxed and alert

Having given the student the support that is needed and the confidence in his own abilities, motivation should be strong. He should have strategies for dealing with the learning process demanded by the education system. Before the examination, teach these learners some relaxation techniques. This is an issue of breathing, to give control over the body, and awareness of muscle tension, particularly if there is a tendency to panic in unfamiliar and stressful situations.

With understanding and sufficient practice, examinations should not be too much of a burden for the majority of dyslexic students. They must be taught to manage their own learning and to keep it on task and to schedule. Success, however, will depend on the level of study skill support and building of self-esteem that the student has received.

Intellectually, these students are as capable as their peers. We need to give them ways to help them show that. Modern languages can present a challenge to students with dyslexia – the strategies suggested by Crombie and McColl (2001) can be useful because they also can be transferred to other subject areas of the curriculum. In other words, they promote good and effective teaching practices which will benefit all learners, especially dyslexic learners.

Some suggestions to help with modern languages are as follows:

- Use charts and diagrams to highlight the bigger picture;
- Add mime and gesture to words;
- Add pictures to text;
- Use colour to highlight gender and accents;
- Label diagrams and charts;
- Use games to consolidate vocabulary;
- Make packs of pocket-size cards; use different colours for different purposes;
- Combine listening and reading by providing text and tape;
- Use Mind Maps© and spidergrams;
- Allow students to produce own tapes;
- Present in small amounts, using a variety of means and with frequent opportunities for repetition and revision;
- Provide an interest in the country – for example, through showing films;
- Rules and other information about the language should be provided in written form for further study and future reference.

As indicated above these are essentially good teaching approaches. It has been long recognised that many of the approaches and strategies for students with dyslexia can benefit all students. This is an important point as it can have implications for staff development and for staff perceptions of the type of support that needs to be offered to students with dyslexia. There are, however, a considerable and increasing range of resources and, particularly, software packages which can be useful for students with dyslexia. Some of these are outlined in the Resources chapter at the end of this book. It is important, however, to recognise that supporting students with dyslexia is not only about providing resources; it is also about acceptance of their learning needs and recognition of the factors associated with curriculum development, differentiation and planning of learning, all of which can help to provide support for students with dyslexia to fulfil their potential in an inclusive educational environment.

Chapter 5

Accessing the Curriculum: Learning Styles and Thinking Skills

It seems reasonable to assume that learning will be more effective when the teaching and the learning environment are compatible with the student's preferred learning style. People learn better when they are able to use their strengths. While this may be a common-sense assumption, it is one of paramount importance for dyslexic children who may not be able to adapt to a teaching style and learning environment that focuses on their weaker modalities. Learning styles, therefore, can be an effective way in which teachers can help dyslexic students access the curriculum. It is important to identify a student's learning style, and also important that the student is made aware of his/her learning style since one of the aims of education is to develop self-sufficiency in learning; to make students autonomous learners. This is especially important if one considers the lifelong aspects of learning and not just the needs of the school curriculum.

The challenge is how to acknowledge the student's individual learning style and still cater for the needs of the whole class, the demands of the curriculum and the sometimes restrictive learning environment. At the very least students can be made aware of their learning styles so that if they are not able to fully utilise them in class they can in their own study at home.

At present there are more than 100 instruments especially designed to identify individual learning styles. Most were developed to evaluate narrow aspects of learning such as the preference for visual, auditory, tactual or kinesthetic input. Others are far more elaborate and focus on factors primarily associated with personality issues such as intuition, active experimentation and reflection (Gregorc 1985; Kolb 1984; Lawrence 1993; McCarthy 1987).

Some perspectives of learning style approaches are briefly described below:

- Riding and Rayner (1998) combine cognitive style with learning strategies. They describe cognitive style as a constraint which includes basic aspects of an individual's psychology such as feeling (affect), doing (behaviour) and knowing (cognition), and the individual's cognitive style relates to how these factors are structured and organised.

- Kolb's (1984) Learning Style Inventory is a derivative of Jung's psychological types combined with Piaget's emphasis on assimilation and accommodation; Lewin's action research model; and Dewey's purposeful, experiential learning. Kolb's 12-item inventory yields four types of learners: divergers, assimilators, convergers and accommodators.

- The Dunn and Dunn approach (Dunn, Dunn and Price 1975) Learning Styles Inventory contains 104 items that produce a profile of learning style preferences in five domains (environmental, emotional, sociological, physiological and psychological) and 21 elements across those domains. These domains and elements include: environmental (sound, light, temperature, design); emotional (motivation, persistence, responsibility, structure); sociological (learning by self, pairs, peers, team, with an adult); physiological (perceptual preference, food and drink intake, time of day, mobility); and psychological (global or analytic preferences, impulsive and reflective).

- Given (1998) constructed a new model of learning styles derived from some key elements of other models. This model consists of emotional learning (the need to be motivated by one's own interests), social learning (the need to belong to a compatible group), cognitive learning (the need to know what age-mates know), physical learning (the need to do and be actively involved in learning), and reflective learning (the need to experiment and explore to find what circumstances work best for new learning).

Learning styles using observational criteria

In addition to using standardised instruments, learning styles may be identified, to a certain extent, through classroom observation. It should be noted that observation in itself may not be sufficient to fully identify learning styles, but the use of a framework for collecting observational data can yield considerable information and can complement the results from more formal assessment.

Observational assessment can be diagnostic, because it is flexible, adaptable and can be used in natural settings with interactive activities. Given and Reid (1999) have developed such a framework – the Interactive Observational Style Identification (IOSI). A summary of this is shown below.

Emotional

Motivation
- What topics, tasks and activities interest the child?
- What kind of prompting and cueing is necessary to increase motivation?
- What kind of incentives motivate the child – leadership opportunities, working with others, free time or physical activity?
- persistence;
- Does the child stick to a task until completion without breaks?
- Are frequent breaks necessary when working on difficult tasks?

Responsibility
- To what extent does the child take responsibility for his/her own learning?
- Does the child attribute success or failure to self or others?

Structure
- Are the child's personal effects (desk, clothing, materials well organised or cluttered?
- How does the child respond to someone imposing organisational structure on him/her?

Social

Interaction
- When is the child's best work accomplished – when working alone, with one another or in a small group?

- Does the child ask for approval or need to have work checked frequently?

Communication
- Does the child give the main events and gloss over the details?
- Does the child interrupt others when they are talking?

Cognitive

Modality preference
- What type of instructions does the child most easily understand – written, oral or visual?
- Does the child respond more quickly and easily to questions about stories heard or read?

Sequential or simultaneous learning
- Does the child begin with one step and proceed in an orderly fashion or have difficulty following sequential information?
- Is there a logical sequence to the child's explanations or do her/his thoughts bounce around from one idea to another?

Impulsive/reflective
- Are the child's responses rapid and spontaneous or delayed and reflective?
- Does the child seem to consider past events before taking action?

Physical
- Does the child move around the class frequently or fidget when seated?
- Does the child like to stand or walk while learning something new?
- Does the child snack or chew on a pencil when studying?
- During which time of day is the child most alert?
- Is there a noticeable difference between morning work completed and afternoon work?

Reflection

Sound
- Does the child seek out places that are particularly quiet?

Light
- Does the child like to work in dimly lit areas or say that the light is too bright?

Temperature
- Does the child leave his/her coat on when others seem warm?

Furniture design
- When given a choice does the child sit on the floor, lie down, or sit in a straight chair to read?

Metacognition
- Is the child aware of his/her learning style strengths?
- Does the child demonstrate internal assessment of self by asking questions such as:
  - Have I done this before?
  - How did I tackle it?
  - What did I find easy?
  - What was difficult?
  - Why did I find it easy or difficult?
  - What did I learn?
  - What do I have to do to accomplish this task?
  - How should I tackle it?
  - Should I tackle it the same way as before?

Prediction
- Does the child make plans and work towards goals or let things happen?

Feedback
- How does the child respond to different types of feedback?
- How much external prompting is needed before the child can access previous knowledge?

There are too many manifestations of style to observe all at once. One way to begin the observation process is to select one of the learning systems and progress from there. The insights usually become greater as observation progresses. Information on learning styles can also be obtained by asking the student questions about his own preferences for learning. This can be achieved with very young children as well as secondary-aged students. Students are usually aware of their own preferences; for example, if they prefer to learn with background music or if they prefer silence when studying.

Metacognitive approaches

Metacognitive approaches can be linked to learning styles. Metacognition essentially means thinking about thinking and by asking questions of the student such as 'How did you do that?', 'Did you use previous knowledge?', 'Have you done that before, how did you tackle it then?' Using this form of self-questioning the teacher can obtain useful information on the student's learning style. This type of self-questioning can help the student identify how a problem could be tackled but also how he/she prefers to learn. It has been indicated in the research (Reid 2003) that children with dyslexic difficulties may have difficulty adapting to different learning environments and for them it is vitally important that their particular learning style is identified and addressed through teaching that matches how they learn. From this, students with dyslexia can gain confidence in their learning abilities and then explore how others like to learn – in a sense, try something new. Perhaps this experimentation and exploration into what learning conditions work best for them are the most important aspects of learning styles being embedded into the curriculum. It is important to reinforce that developing an awareness of learning styles equips students with the skills for lifelong learning.

Thinking skills: a whole-school approach

Students with dyslexia may have difficulty in accessing print but they have little difficulty in solving problems if these are presented to them in an accessible manner. It can be quite frustrating having the ability to deal with problems in, for example, science, history, English, or indeed any subject area, but not getting the opportunity because of the barrier to learning presented by print. Thinking skills are a means of allowing the student to practise problem-solving without having to read vast amounts of information. An example of a thinking skills task is simple decision-making – these are found in the Cort[©] thinking skills progammes, the Somerset thinking skills programmes and the programmes based on 'Instrumental Enrichment' (Feurstein). At a simple level, a problem-solving decision-making task could involve how to spend money and weighing up the different options and the benefits of spending the money on one item as opposed to another. This helps thinking and can provide practice in thinking skills.

Study skills

Similarly, study skills can also help the student with dyslexia practice with different ways of obtaining and retaining information. There are a number of study skills programmes and many study skills exercises can be developed by the subject teacher and contextualised for that subject. Some of the main principles of study skills can include the following:

Organisation of information

It is important that information is organised as the student is learning. Consideration should be given to notetaking to ensure that notes can be packaged into headings and sub-headings – if the student has a page of notes he/she should try to reduce that to five key points and the details of these points can be inserted after each. Students with dyslexia can often do this more effectively using Mind maps© as this is a visual strategy and a strategy that encourages the use of lateral thinking.

It might also be useful for the student to identify one key theme for each page of notes and this key can be noted at the top of the page. This can help in the location of information at the time of revision.

As well as organising their thoughts and the information that is being learnt, students with dyslexia may have to spend some time organising their materials, books, notes and other resources in an accessible way. It is worthwhile spending a little time ensuring information is in folders or box files and perhaps even colour coded. This again will help with the location of information and be time-saving when the information is needed for examination revision. Again, it can be useful for the student to apply labels to various pieces of equipment and to notebooks.

Memory

One of the key aspects of study skills programmes is memory training activities. Students with dyslexia can have a difficulty in short- and long-term memory. To ensure that information is being processed in short-term memory it is necessary to present instructions one at a time, otherwise the information will not be processed. Acknowledging the students learning preference – visual, auditory, kinesthetic and tactile – can be a useful start in relation to ensuring that the information is processed in short-term memory.

Long-term memory can also be problematic for the student with dyslexia and it is important to encourage the student to organise the information throughout learning and revision as this will help information to be retrieved from long-term memory.

The use of mnemonics can also help to retrieve information from long-term memory. There are many examples of well-known mnemonics for music – for example 'every good boy deserves favour' for remembering the treble clef. It is probably more effective, however, if the student develops the mnemonic herself as it will be more meaningful to her.

Memory games can also be useful – games such as matching pairs, eyewitness games and spotting the missing item from a picture or the classroom can all help to train attention, and provide memory practice.

Presentation of information

Students with dyslexia often have difficulty in presenting information, particularly in essay form. The process of writing essays and presenting information in projects should actually be part of a study skills programme. The process of writing – the different stages of investigation in a project and the use of diagrams and other aspects that can illustrate an answer are often overlooked. It is sometimes assumed that if the student knows the content then presentation will be straightforward. This is not the case for students with dyslexia and it is worthwhile spending time developing presentation skills and indeed the process and stages of an investigation or a scientific experiment that may have to be reported on.

Some strategies and stages of essay and report writing are shown below:

Preparation

- Do you understand the question?
- What does the question mean?
- Write down a list of three points;
- What do you already know about these three points?
- Would the three points you have identified answer the question?
- What do you still have to find out? List where you will get this information.

Investigation

- Keep a record of where you obtained information;
- Organise your notes – use headings and sub-headings or Mind maps©;

- Writing notes is an active way of learning, not a passive one – you need to think about the points when you are writing them – ask yourself how what you are writing in your notes answers the question;
- Have you covered all the key points?

Essay plan
- Identify the key points for the introduction;
- Ensure you are discussing each of the key points in different parts of the essay;
- Which examples will you use to support each of your points?
- Conclusion – firm answer to the question;
- Relate to your introduction and the key points you have identified.

Writing the essay
- Limit your sentence length;
- Ensure that each paragraph has a focus (look again at your key points);
- Proofread for meaning then for grammar and spelling;
- Ask yourself if you have said what you intended to.

These three factors – organisation of information; memory, which is retention of information; and presenting of information can form the core of a study skills programme which would be useful for students with dyslexia. It is important, however, to ensure that understanding is not neglected because of this focus on memory strategies. Ideally, an effective memory strategy is one that includes, and indeed enhances, understanding. It is important to ensure that concepts are understood and that these are related to the headings and sub-headings used in reporting. The use of Mind maps©, in fact, helps also to develop concepts and ideas as well as in the retention of information.

The process of learning is important, and especially so with dyslexic students, and it is important to encourage the use of metacognitive strategies which include asking the students to reflect on their own learning – to ask themselves how they did a certain task and whether they could use those strategies again. It is also important to focus on learning styles as well as study skills as these can help the learner develop self-sufficiency in learning and this can prepare the student with dyslexia for lifelong learning.

Chapter 6

Staff Development

One of the key aspects for successful identification and intervention in dyslexia is staff development. It is important that class teachers recognise that staff development in dyslexia is more than a 'quick fix'; it is important for teachers to understand current perceptions, identification procedures and the teaching strategies recognised as being successful for dyslexic students. At the same time it is important to dispel the notion that there is some 'magic' programme for dyslexia – there is not. Many of the successful responses for dyslexia lie in curriculum differentiation and the development of appropriate individual education plans. The key elements of staff development are therefore:

- an awareness of the different aspects related to dyslexia from the biological, cognitive, educational and environmental perspectives;
- examples of dyslexic profiles;
- the academic and emotional needs of dyslexic children;
- the demands placed on them by some subjects;
- curriculum access through differentiation;
- individual education plans – resources and communication with other professionals and parents;
- an acknowledgement of the social and emotional needs of students with dyslexia and the role of self-esteem in successful learning;
- above all, the overall rationale of any school staff development programme should be firmly placed on a whole-school perspective.

Dyslexia research

It is important that teachers have some knowledge of the research underpinning dyslexia which provides the field of dyslexia with credibility and legitimacy. It should not actually be necessary to justify the existence of dyslexia but, unfortunately, it is, as some professionals still have preconceived notions and doubts about the existence of dyslexia. This can be tackled through describing the research from the biological, cognitive, educational and environmental perspectives.

The biological perspective includes:

- aspects relating to the right hemisphere processing style of dyslexic learners;
- the role of the cerebellum which relates to movement and balance;
- the magnocellular system which relates to both visual and auditory discrimination of objects in motion such as when one is scanning from left to right when reading;
- the data which supports the view that there is a hereditablity component to dyslexia, particularly relating to phonological processing.

It is worth emphasising that the biological factors are not fixed – the brain is constantly developing and can be modified by the environment and the learning experiences. It is important that teachers do not get the message that nothing can be done about dyslexia because of these biological factors. Frith (2002) points out that the biological factors interrelate with the other factors and should not be seen in isolation. The interactive aspects are very important as each can influence the other.

The cognitive factors are extremely important as these can have a direct bearing on the effectiveness of learning and this can be influenced to a considerable extent by the teacher. Some of the cognitive factors include:

- role of memory – both short-term and long-term;
- the influence of the information processing cycle – input, cognition and output;
- factors associated with phonological processing;
- metacognition and its importance for learning and study skills;
- automaticity – which includes the need for overlearning as dyslexic children need longer to achieve automaticity.

It is important to emphasise these factors above as they can be the focus of teaching and learning programmes. One other factor which can influence learning and attitude to learning is attribution theory. Burden (2002) suggests that the key question students need to ask is: 'To what do I attribute the successes and failures in my life?' Attribution theory proposes that the reasons people give may be ones which they see as internal to themselves or externally caused by powerful others. Furthermore, such attributions may be seen as changeable or unchangeable, and controllable or uncontrollable. A person with dyslexic difficulties, according to Burden, might attribute those difficulties to lack of ability on their part, which they might also see as unchangeable and outside their control. On the other hand, they might equally well interpret their difficulties as due to inappropriate strategy use, which they might see as changeable and within their control. It is important therefore to highlight the modifiablity of their dyslexic difficulties. This can be done through the use of appropriate strategies but it can also be achieved through curriculum differentiation and support in subject areas. It also emphasises an important role for self-esteem and there may well be scope for specific self-esteem or counselling programmes for dyslexic students. There is a good example of this in a taped interview with a dyslexic student at the Red Rose School for dyslexic children in Lancashire. The student, Philip, was asked how he attributed his improvement in reading and spelling – was it due to the teachers and the school? Interestingly enough, he said that sympathetic teachers and a supportive school was an important factor; he in fact said that the school was the 'most comfortable place he had ever been in, it was like heaven', but the key thing was that it had given him the 'courage' to be an independent learner and take responsibility for his own learning. This is important as it is too easy for students to rely totally on support, which means that any success made is attributed to the support. This implies that it will be difficult for the student to achieve success when the support is no longer in place. That is why it was interesting to hear Philip attribute his success to his 'courage', although clearly the philosophy and support of the school has helped to develop this self-sufficient attitude. But the fact that he does attribute it to himself does mean that the impact of this will extend beyond school and foster a degree of control over the learning process and a positive self-esteem in other areas.

When discussing the factors associated with dyslexia with staff it is important to also note the behavioural characteristics associated with dyslexia. In this context 'behavioural' (educational) means the observed behaviours or characteristics of dyslexia which can be noted by the class teacher. Some of these are outlined in previous chapters in this book but clearly the pattern of spelling errors, reading errors, discrepancies in performances in different subject areas as well as secondary factors such as motivation and attention behavioural difficulties can also be noted.

One of the key factors which needs to be discussed in relation to the background factors associated with dyslexia is the role of the environment, particularly the learning environment. The classroom environment is therefore crucial and there is much evidence from the learning styles field to indicate that by matching the classroom environment and teaching approaches to the learning style of the learner the student's performance can be enhanced. This is discussed in the previous chapter of this book. One of the important aspects related to this is that it implies, as indicated above, that learners take responsibility for their own learning. This is crucial in relation to dyslexia as it minimises the potential for demotivation and learn helplessness that can arise from a feeling of inability to undertake some tasks.

Dyslexic profiles

There is no typical dyslexic profile, but there are characteristics that can be associated with dyslexia. It is possible to present teachers with a profile and suggest that this may be typical, but not all dyslexic children will fall neatly into that profile and this may mislead teachers.

In some of the assessments/tests which can be used, a pattern one might expect to find includes the following:

- low level of general knowledge
- slow processing speed
- can be good verbally
- hesitant in oral reading
- good comprehension
- poor short-term memory
- may have difficulty with long-term memory

- may have coordination difficulties
- may have visual/spatial difficulties
- can be good at music and art
- good problem-solving skills
- may have good social skills and be good at drama
- may have some attention difficulties in certain subjects.

One can note from the list above that it is difficult to discern a typical pattern, but a number of the above characteristics grouped together may constitute a dyslexic profile. There is usually, however, some evidence of discrepancies in different subject areas of the curriculum. That is why communication between teachers in the school is important as it may reveal the extent of this discrepancy and offer some strategies for support.

Academic and social needs

It is important that the academic needs of the student with dyslexia are acknowledged. This may sound fairly obvious but because the dyslexic student may have a considerable difficulty in reading accuracy and fluency these factors may take precedence in a support programme. This may inadvertently be at the cost of developing comprehension and thinking skills.

Curriculum demands and access

The demands placed on the student with dyslexia in different subject areas can fluctuate depending on the particular skills needed for some subjects. For example, it has been noted (Crombie 2002) that modern languages can present the dyslexic student with considerable demands and that this can affect the student's attitude to other subjects and school in general.

Crombie and McColl (2001) suggest that inclusive education carries with it an assumption of entitlement for all those included in the education system. Yet in relation to modern foreign languages for dyslexic students this premise has been ignored. Crombie and McColl argue that 'dyslexic young people, for whatever reason, have been, and still are, on occasions removed from the modern languages classroom to work elsewhere being considered unable to benefit from the work taking place'. They suggest that access to the modern languages curriculum through use of appropriate strategies is at times denied the dyslexic student, and they comment on the historical trend ranging from the view of the innate nature of language skills to the current emphasis on real-life language for real-life situations, with an emphasis on speaking and listening and collaborative teaching. Although learning foreign languages may still not be easy for dyslexic students, with the appropriate understanding, curriculum, techniques and support, Crombie and McColl suggest it should be possible. This, of course, like other subject areas has considerable time implications for subject teachers and for the school management in terms of timetable considerations. Time needs to be allocated for this type of planning and developing of dyslexia-friendly materials which will, in the long run, be cost-effective, as these will be useful for all students.

Areas of difficulty, such as phonological processing, working memory, auditory discrimination, auditory sequencing and confusion over grammar and syntax, can still be problematic for dyslexic students, yet many of the strategies which have been successfully used for dyslexic students to improve their literacy in English can also be used for second-language learning. Indeed many of the techniques involving overlearning and the use of multi-sensory strategies can help with developing phonological awareness and grammar skills for all students.

This provides a challenge for teachers and support staff to identify the strengths of dyslexic students and to ensure that the content of the modern languages curriculum and, indeed, the curriculum in other subject areas is presented in a manner that can be accessed by dyslexic students.

It can be suggested that a totally inclusive curriculum, which will benefit dyslexic students, needs to be approached from a whole-school perspective.

The criteria for the curriculum objectives and the key concepts of each subject area need to be identified and this also includes the criteria on assessment. Tod and Fairman (2001) propose the view that teachers have broadly welcomed a government commitment to inclusion but there is still some concern about whether the ideologies of inclusion can be realised for all individuals, particularly in view of the competitive educational contexts which appear to dominate educational outcomes. Garner and Gains (2000) suggest that the almost exclusive emphasis on subject knowledge and standard forms of assessment make full curriculum access very difficult for some students.

This has implications for cross-curriculum factors. Kirk (2001) explores some of the criteria for cross-curriculum factors in secondary schools through the implementation of staff development. She suggests that the adoption of cross-curricular approaches needs to focus on some basic concerns about the subject-based curriculum and the misleading assumption that each subject area has a separate contribution to make to the education of every pupil. Kirk acknowledges that the current focus on cross-curricular themes should help to redress this imbalance and prevent the potential of a fragmented learning experience for students.

It is important, according to Kirk, that the common features which all subjects share should be exploited in both curriculum development and in teaching. Kirk summarises this view by suggesting that 'the teaching of a subject does not simply involve the transmission of content that is taken for granted; but, on the contrary, it involves a careful examination of how the subjects in their different ways contribute to the wider educational and social purposes of the secondary school'. This view clearly has implications for inclusion, for staff development and full curricular access for dyslexic students.

Individual education plans

Tod and Fairman (2001) suggest that it is difficult for some students with dyslexia to understand whether topics are compartmentalised or interlinked. To overcome this dyslexic students need to be aware of the whole syllabus and how each of the component parts fits into the whole. It has been noted (Reid 1998, 2003) that dyslexic children tend to have a preference for learning in a holistic manner. This means that they will benefit from seeing the whole first and then the individual components. This holistic framework is essential for the development of a schema of the subject area and for the development of concepts.

Tod and Fairman suggest that students who experience problems with organisation or in conceptualising time may feel de-skilled because they do not have 'the whole picture'. A clear understanding of the relative importance of different aspects of the subject area can help them prioritise their work. This can have implications for Group Education Plans as well as individual plans.

Tod and Fairman maintain that individual plans should be contextualised in order to identify 'additional or different provision'

to that given to all pupils and should be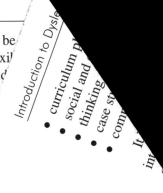
level. Schools, they suggest, need flexi
that the specific needs of dyslexic stu
targets, therefore, should reflect the n
social aspects of development; sho
should be concerned with both acces
and should address both skills and
individual planning should be both
as purposeful and motivating.

Whole-school policies

It is important, therefore, that schools have a whole-school policy on
dyslexia. It is too easy to delegate a member of staff with the
responsibility for dyslexia. While there are advantages to having a
delegated and dedicated member of staff for dyslexia there are also
dangers that the rest of the staff may feel de-skilled in relation to
dealing with dyslexic difficulties and shift responsibility to the
'specialist'. This can be counter-productive as it may inadvertently
prevent the subject or class teacher taking responsibility for
differentiation and ensuring the needs of dyslexic students are
considered in curriculum planning and assessment.

Approaches to staff development

There are implications throughout this chapter for staff development,
but the nature of that staff development is a crucial factor. All too
often schools undertake staff development in dyslexia almost on an
ad hoc basis, hoping to obtain some quick-fix strategies for all staff.
Instead, staff development needs to be planned with a programme
stretching over time. There needs to be perhaps one session, allowing
teachers to provide feedback that can inform subsequent sessions.

A possible programme for staff development may include some of
the following:

- What is dyslexia? – descriptions, definitions, research background;
- identifying dyslexia – assessment criteria for different subjects,
  observational assessment;
- teaching strategies;
- curriculum differentiation in different subject areas;

anning, targets and assessment;

motional factors, self-esteem, peer learning;

skills, metacognition, learning styles;

dies, profiles and pointers and examples of action;

nunication – parents, professionals, school staff.

is particularly crucial that the above programme is not incorporated o a 'crash course' in dyslexia – rather it should be seen as at least a ne-session course. There are many competing demands on staff development time, particularly staff development involving the whole staff, but it should be acknowledged that the benefits of staff development in the area of dyslexia may have beneficial spin-off effects for other areas and the teaching and learning of all pupils in all subjects.

Issues and considerations for staff development

It is important also to consider some of the issues relating to staff development and how these can be addressed in relation to the implementation of a staff development programme such as the one above.

Kirk (2001) refers to the work of O'Sullivan, Jones and Reid (1988) who offer two contrasting models of staff development. One involves an almost ad hoc programme which is directed by the management, with little teacher involvement. Usually this type of staff development is voluntary and teachers select from a menu of options. This can lead to a fragmented approach although some teachers may see this menu-type offering as being more relevant. This, however, may be short-sighted as some subject specialists may not see the relevance of staff development on dyslexia, and will not select this option.

A contrasting approach discussed by Kirk refers to a bottom-up process for identifying staff development needs which would stem from the teachers themselves. The main focus would be the curriculum and not individual subjects needs. In this way the needs of all pupils would be regarded, and monitoring and evaluation would be an integral part of the staff development process.

Summary

To summarise, this chapter has suggested that staff development should engage the views and needs of subject and class teachers. In addition to providing an understanding of dyslexia, staff development should also provide the opportunities for curriculum development in relation to the needs of the dyslexic student as well as the actual subject area. Participants of a staff development programme should be provided with:

- a sound framework of the theoretical issues relating to dyslexia;
- a critical awareness of assessment, teaching and curriculum issues;
- an awareness of relevant research and an understanding that knowledge in this area is continually developing;
- an ability to link ongoing research with practice;
- experience and competence in practical aspects relating to the identification and teaching of learners with dyslexia;
- an awareness of the holistic dimensions associated with dyslexia including social and emotional factors, parental involvement, multi-disciplinary approaches including the role of other professionals;
- whole-school issues including assessment, examinations, time-tabling, learning styles and curriculum differentiation.

The emphasis in this chapter is therefore on a broader conceptual definition of dyslexia and the ways in which it can be addressed by teachers within the context of the curriculum and the school.

Chapter 7

Resources

There is a vast amount of resources that can be accessed to support students with dyslexia. The following suggestions are a sample of some of these that may be relevant for all age groups, depending on individual literacy and numeracy levels.

Software

1. General principles when choosing software
- Consider the reading and spelling ages and interest levels of the learners.
- Is the learner receiving specialist dyslexia tuition? If so, there may be a program related to, or that will complement, the teaching scheme being used.
- Good software is structured, progressive, cumulative and motivating.
- It is easy for users to find their way around the options in good software.
- Good software is interactive and encourages users to try the tasks.
- It is always best to use programs that have speech support, especially in literacy.
- It is usually best to work through tasks in the suggested program order.
- It is helpful to have software that keeps records of users' progress.

2. Phonic reading and spelling
Wordshark 3. Interactive demo disk available (available from White Space Ltd, 41 Mall Road, London W6 9DG, www.wordshark.co.uk).

It contains the most useful words from all the lists in teaching schemes such as Alpha to Omega and National Literacy High Frequency words at Primary level. Lists can be modified or the student's own words entered. Many alphabet, reading, spelling, sentence- and word-splitting activities with optional difficulty and speed levels in 36 games. Detailed records are kept of the student's progress. This is important as the student, especially students with dyslexia, needs to see that they are actually making progress. This is vital for motivation and self-esteem. Wordshark 3 is designed to run on high-specification PCs and Windows 98 or above. Wordshark 2L is still available for users of older PCs.

The catch-up CD-ROM. Multimedia activities and games to help users learn to read and spell the first 100 high-frequency words using five themed worlds that will appeal to children.

Bangor range of software for Acorn and 4 titles for PC. Different programs with interesting variety for reading and spelling of each level of phonics, based on the Bangor Dyslexia Unit teaching scheme. Some of the programs have a number of ways of reinforcing the words: Chatback; Sounds and Rhymes; Magic E; Soapbox; Punctuate.

3. For spelling mainly

Starspell 2001. The classic 'Look (Hear & Say), Cover, Write and Check' routine with two other activities and optional pictorial support. After practising, a good option is to hear the word without seeing it. Good phonic lists, onset and rime, National Literacy Hour words, a wide range of curriculum vocabulary and context sentences. Own words. Excellent speech. Printable worksheets. Detailed user records.

4. For reinforcement after learning several word families

Gamz Player. A computerised version of their 28 SWAP card games, with a good handbook, quick user guide and other activities. You can customise the sets and enter your own words.

5. Talking books

Hearing the words as you see them makes the experience multi-sensory, which helps dyslexic learners. Users can access the texts at a pace and interest level that suits them, and can follow the text being read.

6. Adventure programs

These may be designed for maths or other subjects, but they also require reading, decision-making, and remembering.

7. Talking encyclopaedias

Masses of information, often with animations, web links and video clips. They are easy to navigate by clicking on internal links. Encyclopaedias without speech can be accessed through text reading software such as textHELP® and Penfriend. The features of textHELP® are read-back speech facility, word prediction – with phonetic and grammar-based predictions, Word Wizard to help search for words and phonetic spellchecker with integrated thesaurus.

8. Word-processors

- Word-processing programs have made a major difference to many dyslexic learners.
- They can help with writing in education, work and leisure activities.
- They can be helpful for supporting the writing process (getting your ideas organised), and also for those who find presentation or handwriting a problem.
- Word-processing is a key written communication tool used in schools, colleges and many work situations.
- Word-processing enables easy drafting and editing. Users can move written text around the page easily, using facilities such as delete, cut, copy and paste. Dyslexic learners don't have to worry about rewriting texts many times over to get a neat piece of writing.
- Word-processed text always looks pleasing. It is easier for their teachers to read too.
- It is particularly helpful in schools and colleges when pupils and students can type longer pieces of work or essays.
- Font size, colour and style can be changed easily.
- Underline, **bold** and *italic* are simple but effective tools.
- Often additional features such as borders, clipart and tables can be added to text.
- It can be useful to use the same word-processing software at home as that used in school or work.
- Some users type very slowly. Using additional wordbanks, grids or predictive programs can help enter text more quickly (see items 12 and 13 below).

9. Talking word-processors

Talking word-processors have a speech facility that enables users to hear the words and sentences as they are being typed. They use synthesised (robotic sounding) speech. This can help accuracy and reassure users that the content makes sense. Many offer a range of voices to choose from. They are used in many schools, especially at KS1, 2 and 3. Some will read toolbars and spellchecking menus, e.g. **Textease**, **Write:OutLoud**. Some talking word-processors have an on-screen wordbank facility.

10. Spellcheckers

Spellcheckers in word-processors can help identify misspellings or typing errors. However, many computer spellcheckers are not very helpful when suggesting a correction list. They usually suggest words that have the first two letters in the spelling error. If these letters are wrong it *may not* suggest the word needed, e.g. type 'sercle' and 'serial' or 'serve' may be the corrections suggested. A hand-held Spellchecker (*Franklin*) may be useful. Talking word-processor, **Write:OutLoud**, incorporates a Franklin Spellchecker. Facilities such as 'search and replace', however, will find repeated errors and correct them. The error (e.g. 'thay') and corrected version ('they') need only be typed once and the other corrections will be done automatically.

11. Quicktionary Reading Pen

Scan a word from any printed text. See the word displayed in large characters. Hear the word read aloud from the built-in speaker or from headphones. Display the definition of the word with one push of a button. Battery-operated (*iANSYST*).

12. Additional on-screen wordbanks and grids

Additional on-screen wordbanks and grids usually have their own speech facility enabling users to hear the words. They can offer multiple lists of words or phrases on screen, for use with the word-processor. Users click on the word or phrase and it is typed automatically into the word-processor. Pictures and recorded speech can be added to some wordbanks. These Wordbanks enable text to be entered quickly and accurately and help users with difficult or subject-specific spellings. Users can create their own grids of words for personal or subject use. The Crick programs have many useful ones ready made for their users, for all key stages that can be downloaded free from their website.

13. Predictive programs

Predictive programs can be used to help cut down keystrokes, save typing time and aid spelling. The program tries to suggest from one or two keystrokes what the user is trying to type from common or regularly used words. It presents the suggestions in a window on the screen where the user can listen and then make the appropriate choice, e.g. type the letter 't' and up to 8 or 9 common words are suggested, such as: 'the, this, there, they', etc. Many of these programs have a speech facility enabling the word-processor to talk (**Penfriend XP, Co:Writer 4000, textHELP!, Read & Write**).

14. Typing and keyboard skills

To make full use of word-processing it is helpful to develop efficient and accurate keyboard and typing skills. There are a number of programs which include keyboard skills.

15. Voice or speech recognition software

Voice or speech recognition software enables users to speak the words they want to word-process. This may be a useful option especially for older pupils, students and adults. However, it may be not as easy as it sounds. It takes time and training.

16. BDA ICT booklets

These booklets are available from the British Dyslexia Association, 98 London Road, Reading RG1 5AU, UK, and are written and presented in a user-friendly manner.

Mathematics

Books

Agnew, M., Barlow, S., Davies, O., Pascal, L., Skidmore, S. (1995) *Get Better Grades with Maths*. London: Piccadilly Press (ISBN 1-85340-392-X).

Chinn, S. J. (1996) *What to Do When You Can't Learn the Times Tables*. Baldock: Egon Publishers. (also available as a CD-ROM *REM*)

Chinn, S. J. (1998) *Sum Hope: Breaking the Numbers Barrier*. London: Souvenir Press.

Chinn, S. J. (1999) *What To Do When You Can't Add and Subtract*. Baldock: Egon Publishers.

Chinn, S. J. and Ashcroft, L. R. (1998) *Mathematics for Dyslexics: A teaching handbook* (2nd edn). London: Whurr.

Miles, T. R. and Miles, E. (eds) (1992) *Dyslexia and Mathematics*. London: Routledge.
Robson, P. (1995) *Maths Dictionary*. Newby Books (ISBN 1-872682-18-4).

Maths study and question books for all key stages
CGP (Tel. 0870 750 1262).
Henderson, A. (1989) *Maths and Dyslexia*. St David's College, Llandudno.
Using ICT to Support Mathematics in Primary Schools (training pack available only to schools). DfES (0845 60 222 60) (Ref. 0260/2000)
IANS: The Informal Assessment of Numeracy Skills.
Available from Mark College (www.markcollege.somerset.sch.uk)

Software for maths
Numbershark-PC. (KS1–3) Numbershark is by the makers of Wordshark and has the same type of colourful, fun graphics in structured learning tasks and a similar range of enjoyable reward games. It covers number recognition and sorting and the four main rules of number, i.e. addition, subtraction, multiplication and division. The actual numbers are represented in the games, as words, in a numberline, as rods, in digits, on an abacus, in a scale, and on a numberpad, which provides variety. Dyslexic pupils who have problems with short-term memory, sequencing skills and short attention span love this software and the 30 different activities. It gives them the chance to build up confidence, and the opportunity to practise and try out those aspects of number that worry them, in an easily accessible way. Study of the manual by the supervising adult is essential as there are so many options.

It is important to choose useful levels and to work through the teaching and practise activities as well as applying them in the games. (White Space Ltd, demo disk available. Tel/Fax: 020 8748 5927; e-mail: sales@wordshark.co.uk; www.wordshark.co.uk)

Maths Circus Act 1. PC, Acorn, Mac (KS1–3) Twelve different games can be played and each one has five levels of difficulty. All the puzzles require reasoning skills. There are straightforward instructions. Players simply press an arrow to work through the different levels of the package. The colourful graphics relate to circus life with seals, lions, high wire acts, etc. A simple colour-coded record is kept of each player's progress. They can log on with their special player code and tackle additional tasks. The early levels can be solved by trial and error but learners gain the greatest benefit if they verbalise their reasons for following a procedure to solve a puzzle. For teachers there is also a useful set of 24 activity sheets which can be photocopied. There are now Maths Circus Acts 2 & 3 for those who have cracked the first set of puzzles. (4Mation, tel: 01271 325 353; fax: 01271 322 974; e-mail: sales@4mation.co.uk; www.4mation.co.uk)

MathMania PC. Acorn. (KS2–4) Navigate through a maze finding a key and reaching the exit with the required score. Score points by collecting gold bars or by answering questions to get through barriers. Once each maze is completed, a puzzle appears and then another maze. There are four levels of difficulty for the questions, which can be set on number, time, measurement, shape and space or a mixture of all these in a lucky dip. It is possible for teachers to edit the question bank. Pupils enjoy this program as it is simple to use and fits well into a short lesson. The questions vary from simple sums, like 5 + 8, to the equivalent in words. The latter is most useful as this is an area that causes great problems in maths. MathMania is simple and effective and good value. (Topologika Demo download and on CD-ROM, tel: 01326 377 771; fax: 01326 376 755; e-mail: sales@topologika.com; www.topologika.co.uk)

Chefren's Pyramid. (KS3) This will challenge the whole family and this adventure can easily become addictive. You have become separated from your group on a tour of the Pyramids and have to find your own way out, passing through a series of rooms as you go. To move through a room you must answer all its questions correctly. If you make more than one mistake, you are dropped back to the room below! You can save your position to return on another occasion. The questions start with simple single figure addition and move upwards through many different mathematical topics, mostly suitable to KS3 learners. Ideally this program will provide a means for parents to work with their children. For older 'children' there is also Cheop's Pyramid. (Nicholl Education Limited, tel: 01484 860 006; fax: 01484 860 008; e-mail: admin@nicholl.co.uk; www.pyramid-maths.com)

BDA ICT Booklets.
Catch 'em Young (early learners).
Count on Your Computer. Ideas and suggestions for using technology to support maths and numeracy (for all key stages).

Creative writing

Inspiration is a software program to help the student develop ideas and organise thinking. Through the use of diagrams it helps the student comprehend concepts and information. Essentially the use of diagrams can help to make creating and modifying concept maps and ideas easier. The user can also prioritise and rearrange ideas, helping with essay-writing. Inspiration can therefore be used for brainstorming, organising, pre-writing, concept mapping, planning and outlining. There are 35 in-built templates and these can be used for a range of subjects including English, history and science. Dyslexic people often think in pictures rather than words. This technique can be used for note-taking, for remembering information and organising ideas for written work. The inspiration program converts this image into a linear outline. The program is available from: iANSYST Ltd, The White House, 72 Fen Road, Cambridge CB4 1UN (tel: 01223 42 01 01; fax: 01223 42 66 44; e-mail: sales@dyslexic.com) (supply excellent reading and spelling computer programmes suitable for dyslexic students).

Motivation

Start to Finish Books. This series of books (Don Johnston, 18 Clarendon Court, Calver Road, Winwick Quay, Warrington WA2 8QP, tel: 01925 241642; fax: 01925 241745; www.donjohnston.com), can be beneficial as the series, designed to boost reading and comprehension skills, provides a reader profile, a computer book, audio cassette and paperback book. Designed to engage children in reading real literature, the series can help with fluency and motivation. Some of the topics included in the series are: history, famous people, sports, original mysteries and re-tellings of classic literature. Don Johnston also produce some excellent software for children with literacy difficulties. This includes **Write: OutLoud3** (discussed above). This program supports each step of the writing process including: generating ideas – helps with brainstorming and researching topics; expressing ideas – this allows children to hear their words as they write; editing work – using a spellchecker designed to check for phonetic misspellings; revising for meaning – helps with word-finding and improves written expression.

Reading fluency

The Hi-Lo readers from LDA, Cambridge and other similar books, such as those from Barrington Stoke Ltd, 10 Belford Terrace, Edinburgh EH4 3DQ, can be beneficial in relation to motivation. These books, particularly those from Barrington Stoke, have been written with the reluctant reader in mind and they can help students with dyslexia with reading fluency, in maintaining reading comprehension and generally developing processing speed. Barrington Stoke have also a series of books devoted to teenage fiction.

Penfriend. This software, from Design Concept, 30 South Oswald Road, Edinburgh EH9 2HG (tel: 0131 668 2000; www.jasper.co.uk/penfriend) provides an excellent word prediction tool and also has an on-screen keyboard specifically aimed at children with dyslexia and writing difficulties. It also provides three lexicons for different ages, and new word lists for different topics can be created.

Teaching reading

Toe by Toe Multisensory Manual for Teachers and Parents (Keda Cowling, available from Keda Publications, 17 Heatherside, Baildon, West Yorks BD17 5LG, tel: 01274 588278). Toe by Toe is a multi-sensory teaching method highly recommended for teachers and parents. The programme has a multi-sensory element, a phonic element some focus on the student's memory through the planning and the timing of each of the lessons in the book. It can be used readily by parents and the instructions are very clear.

Stride Ahead – An Aid to Comprehension (Keda Cowling) can be a useful follow-up to Toe by Toe. Essentially, Stride Ahead has been written for children who can read but may have difficulty in understanding what they are reading. (Available from Keda Publications, 17 Heatherside, Baildon, West Yorkshire, BD17 5LG, tel/fax: 01274 588278.)

Interactive Literacy Games (Crossbow Education, 41 Sawpit Lane, Brocton, Stafford ST17 0TE, www.crossboweducation.com). Crossbow Education specialises in games for children with dyslexia and produce activities on literacy, numeracy and study skills. These include 'Spingoes' and onset and rime spinner bingo which comprises a total of 120 games using onset and rime; 'Funics' a practical handbook of activities to help children to recognise and use rhyming words, blend and segment syllables, identify initial phonemes and link sounds to symbols. 'Funics' is produced by Maggie Ford and Anne Tottman and is available from Crossbow Education. Crossbow also produce literacy games including Alphabet Lotto, which focuses on early phonics, 'Bing-Bang-Bong' and 'CVC Spring', which help develop competence in short vowel sounds and 'Deebees', a stick and circle board game to deal with b/d confusion. They also have board games called 'Magic-E', 'Spinit' and 'Hotwords', a five board set for teaching and reinforcing 'h' sounds such as 'wh', 'sh', 'ch', 'th', 'ph', 'gh' and silent 'h'. 'Oh No', a times table photocopiable game book, and 'tens 'n' units', which consists of spinning board games which help children of all ages practise the basics of place value in addition and subtraction.

Staff Development

BDA Handbook, published annually by the BDA, 98 London Road, Reading RG1 5AU.

Fawcett, A. (ed.) (2001) *Dyslexia: Theory and Good Practice.* London: Whurr Publishers.

Peer, L. and Reid, G. (eds) (2000) *Multilingualism, Literacy and Dyslexia.* London: David Fulton Publishers.

Peer, L. and Reid, G. (eds) (2001) *Successful Inclusion in the Secondary School.* London: David Fulton Publishers.

Reid, G. (2003) *Dyslexia*: *A Practitioner's Handbook* (3rd edn). Chichester: Wiley.

Reid, G. and Kirk, J. (2001) *Dyslexia in Adults.* Chichester: Wiley.

Reid, G. and Wearmouth, J. (2002) (eds) *Dyslexia and Literacy*: *Theory and Practice.* Chichester: Wiley.

Website links

Adult Dyslexia Organisation
    (www.futurenet.co.uk/charity/ado/index.html)
Arts Dyslexia Trust (www.sniffout.net/home/adt)
British Dyslexia Association (www.bda-dyslexia.org.uk/)
Creative Learning Company New Zealand
    (www.creativelearningcentre.com)
Dr Gavin Reid (www.gavinreid.co.uk)
Dyslexia Association of Ireland (www.acld-dyslexia.com)

Dyslexia Institute (www.dyslexia-inst.org.uk)
Dyslexia Research Trust (www.dyslexic.org.uk)
Dyslexia in Scotland (www.dyslexia-in-scotland.org)
European Dyslexia Academy for Research and Training E-DART
   (www.psyk.uu.se/edart/)
Helen Arkell Dyslexia Centre (www.arkellcentre.org.uk)
Hornsby International Dyslexia Centre (www.hornsby.co.uk)
I am dyslexic – a site put together by an 11 year old dyslexic boy –
   (www.iamdyslexic.com)
Institute for Neuro-Physiological Psychology (INPP)
   (www.inpp.org.uk)
International Dyslexia Association (IDA) (www.interdys.org)
Learning and Behaviour Charitable Trust New Zealand
   (www.lbctnz.co.nz)
Mark College (www.markcollege.somerset.sch.uk)
Mind-field (www.mind-field.org)
PATOSS (www.patoss-dyslexia.org)
Quantum Learning (www.trainthebrain.co.uk)
Red Rose School and Dyslexia North West
   (www.dyslexiacentre.com)
School Daily New Zealand (www.schooldaily.com)

ICT suppliers

iANSYST (www.dyslexic.com)
Crick Software (www.cricksoft.co.uk)
Inclusive Technology (www.inclusive.co.uk)
SEMERC (www.blackcatsoftware.com)
Xavier Educational Software (www.xavier.bangor.ac.uk)

This chapter has provided an overview of some of the resources that
may be suitable particularly for the student with dyslexia in the
secondary school. Many of these, however, are also appropriate for
primary-aged children, but the important point is that age-appropriate
materials need to be used for the student in secondary school even if
his/her reading age is at a primary level. This can be more motivating
for the student and can enhance the possibility of success in each area of
the curriculum. It is important to recognise, however, that the barriers to
learning experienced by many students with dyslexia can be overcome
not only with the use of resources but through teacher and management
awareness, curriculum planning and staff development.

References and Further Reading

Badian, N. A. (1997) 'Dyslexia and the double deficit hypothesis', *Annals of Dyslexia*, **47**.

Bakker, D. (1998) 'Balance model'. Paper read at the 13th All Polish Conference, Polish Dyslexia Association, University of Gdansk, Poland.

Bakker, D. and Robertson, J. (2002) 'The balance model of reading', in Reid, G. and Wearmouth, J. (eds) *Dyslexia and Literacy*. Chichester: Wiley.

Bakker, D. J., Licht, R. and Kappers, E. J. (1994) 'Hemispheric stimulation techniques in children with dyslexia', in Tramontana, M. G. and Hooper, S. R. (eds) *Advances in Child Neuropsychology*, Vol. 3. New York: Springer Verlag.

BDA (1999) Dyslexia Friendly Schools Resource Pack. Reading: British Dyslexia Association.

Biggar, S. and Barr, J. (1996) 'The emotional world of specific learning difficulties', in Reid, G. (ed.) *Dimensions of Dyslexia*. Edinburgh: Moray House Publications.

BPS (1999) 'Dyslexia, Literacy and Psychological Assessment'. Report by a working party of the Division of Educational and Child Psychology of the British Psychological Society. Leicester: British Psychological Society.

Brooks, R. B. (2001) 'Fostering motivation, hope, and resilience in children with learning disorders', *Annals of Dyslexia*, **51**.

Brown, A., Armbruster, B. and Baker, L. (1986) 'The role of metacognition in reading and studying', in Oraspinu, J. (ed.) *Reading Comprehension From Research to Practice*. Hillsdale, NJ: Lawrence Erlbaum.

Burden, B. (2002) 'A cognitive approach to dyslexia: learning styles and thinking skills', in Reid, G. and Wearmouth, J. (eds) *Dyslexia and Literacy: Theory and Practice*. Chichester: Wiley.

Crombie, M. (2002) 'Dealing with diversity in the primary classroom: a challenge for the class teacher', in Reid, G. and Wearmouth, J. (eds) *Dyslexia and Literacy: Theory and Practice*. Chichester: Wiley.

Crombie, M. and McColl, H. (2001) 'Dyslexia and the teaching of modern foreign languages', in Peer, L. and Reid, G. (eds) *Dyslexia: Successful Inclusion in the Secondary School*. London: David Fulton.

Curry, L. (1990) *Learning Styles in Secondary School: A review of instruments and implications for their use*. Ottawa, Ontario, Canada: Curry Adams and Associates, Inc.

Dennison, P. E. and Dennison, G. E. (1989) *Brain Gym* (Teacher's edition revised). Ventura, CA: Edu-Kinesthetics, Inc.

Dobie, S. (1998) Personal correspondence.

Dunn, R., Dunn, K. and Price, G. E. (1975). *Learning Style Inventory*. Lawrence, KS: Price Systems.

Dunn, R., Griggs, S., Olson, J., Beasley, M. and Gorman, B. (1995). 'A meta-analytic validation of the Dunn and Dunn model of learning-style preferences', *Journal of Educational Research*, **88**(61), 353–62.

East Renfrewshire Council (1999) *Dyslexia, Policy on Specific Learning Difficulties*. East Renfrewshire Council, Scotland.

Eden, G. F., Van Meter, J. W., Rumsey, J. M., Maisog, J. M., Woods, R. P. and Zeffiro, T.A. (1996) 'Abnormal processing of visual motion in dyslexia revealed by functional brain imaging', *Nature*, **382**, 67–9.

Everatt, J. (2002) 'Visual processes', in Reid, G. and Wearmouth, J. (eds) *Dyslexia and Literacy: Theory and Practice*. Chichester: Wiley.

Fawcett, A. J. and Nicolson, R. I. (1992) 'Automatisation deficits in balance for dyslexic children', *Perceptual and Motor Skills*, **75**, 507–29.

Fawcett, A. J. and Nicolson, R. I. (1996) *The Dyslexia Screening Test*. London: The Psychological Corporation.

Fawcett, A. J. and Nicolson, R. I. (1997) *The Dyslexia Early Screening Test*. London: The Psychological Corporation.

Fawcett, A. J., Nicolson, R. I. and Dean, P. (1996) 'Impaired performance of children with dyslexia on a range of cerebellar tasks'. *Annals of Dyslexia*, **46**.

Fawcett, A. J. and Nicolson, R. I. (1998) *Dyslexia Adult Screening Test*. London: The Psychological Corporation.

Fife Education Authority (1996) *Partnership: Parents, professionals and pupils*. Glenrothes: Fife Education Authority.

Flavell, J. H. (1979) 'Metacognition and cognitive monitoring', *American Psychologist*, October, 906–11.

Fredrickson, N., Frith, U. and Reason, R. (1997) *Phonological Assessment Battery*. Windsor: NFER-Nelson.

Frith, U. (2002) 'Resolving the paradoxes of dyslexia', in Reid, G. and Wearmouth, J. (eds) *Dyslexia and Literacy: Theory and Practice*. Chichester: Wiley.

Galaburda, A. (ed.) (1993) *Dyslexia and Development: Neurological aspects of extraordinary brains*. Cambridge, MA: Harvard University Press.

Garner, P. and Gains, C. (2000) 'The debate that never happened'. *Special*, Autumn, 8–9.

Given, B. K. (1998) 'Psychological and neurobiological support for learning-style instruction: why it works', *National Forum of Applied Educational Research Journal*, **11**(1), 10–15.

Given, B. K. and Reid, G. (1999) 'The interactive observation style identification', in Given, B. K. and Reid, G. *Learning Styles: A guide for teachers and parents*. St Anne's on Sea: Red Rose Publications.

Goleman, D. (1995) *Emotional Intelligence*. New York: Bantam.

Gregorc, A. F. (1985) *Inside Styles: Beyond the Basics*. Columbia, CT: Gregorc Assoc. Inc.

Gregorc, Diane F. (1997) *Relating to Style*. Columbia, CT: Gregorc Associates, Inc.

Grinder, M. (1991) *Righting the Educational Conveyor Belt* (2nd edn). Portland, OR: Metamorphous Press.

Hagtvet, B. E. (1997) 'Phonological and linguistic-cognitive precursors of reading abilities', *Dyslexia*, **3**(3).

Hatcher, P. (1994) *Sound Linkage*. London: Whurr.

Horne, J. K., Singleton, C. H. and Thomas, K. V. (1999) *Lucid Assessment System for Schools*, (*secondary version*) (LASS secondary). Beverley: Lucid Creative Limited.

Hulme, C. and Snowling, M. (1997) *Dyslexia: Biology, Cognition and Intervention*. London: Whurr.

Johanson, K. (1997) 'Sound therapy'. Paper presented at the Fourth International Conference, BDA, York.

Johnson, M., Philips, S. and Peer, L. (1999) Multisensory Teaching System for Reading. Special Educational Needs Centre, Didsbury School of Education, Manchester Metropolitan University.

Kirk, J. (2001) 'Cross-curricular approaches to staff development in secondary schools', in Peer, L. and Reid, G. *Dyslexia: Successful Inclusion in the Secondary School*. London: David Fulton Publishers.

Kolb, D. (1984) *Experiential Learning: Experience as the source of learning and development*. Englewood Cliffs, NJ: Prentice-Hall.

Lawrence, G. (1979/1982/1993) *People Types and Tiger Stripes* (3rd edn). Gainsville, FL: Center for Applications of Psychological Type, Inc.

Lazear, D. (1991) *Seven Ways of Knowing*. Palatine, IL: Skylight Publishing.

Lazear, D. (1999) *Eight Ways of Knowing: Teaching for multiple intelligences*. Arlington Heights, IL: Skylight Professional Development.

McCarthy, B. (1980/1987) *The 4mat System: Teaching to learning styles with right/left mode techniques*. Barrington, IL.

MacKay, N. (2001) 'Dyslexia friendly schools', in Peer, L. and Reid, G. (eds) *Dyslexia: Successful Inclusion in the Secondary School*. London: David Fulton.

McPherson of Cluny (1999) (The McPherson Report). The Stephen Lawrence Inquiry. London: Home Office.

McPhillips, M., Hepper, P. G. and Mulhern, G. (2000) 'Effects of replicating primary–reflex movements on specific reading difficulties in children: a randomised double-blind, controlled trial', *The Lancet*, **355**, 537–41.

Miles, T. R. (1983) *Bangor Dyslexia Test*. Cambridge: Learning Development Aids.

Montgomery, D. (1998) *Reversing Lower Attainment: Developing Curriculum Strategies for Overcoming Disaffection and Underachievement*. London: David Fulton Publishers, p. 38.

Murray-Harvey, R. (1994) 'Conceptual and measurement properties of the productivity environmental preference survey as a measure of learning style', *Educational and Psychological Measurement*, **54**(4), 1002–12.

Muter, V., Hulme, C. and Snowling, M. (1997) *Phonological Abilities Test*. London: Psychological Corporation.

Nicolson, R. (2001) 'Developmental dyslexia: into the future', in Fawcett, A. (ed.) *Dyslexia Theory and Good Practice*. London: Whurr.

O'Sullivan, F., Jones, K. and Reid, K. (1988) *Staff Development in Secondary Schools*. London: Hodder and Stoughton.

Peer, L. (2001) 'Dyslexia and its manifestations in the secondary school', in Peer, L. and Reid, G. (eds) *Dyslexia: Successful Inclusion in the Secondary School*. London: David Fulton Publishers.

Peer, L. and Reid, G. (eds) (2000) *Multilingualism, Literacy and Dyslexia: A challenge for educators*. London: David Fulton Publishers.

Peer, L. and Reid, G. (eds) (2001) *Dyslexia: Successful Inclusion in the Secondary School*. London: David Fulton Publishers.

Pumfrey, P. (1996) 'Specific developmental dyslexia: basics to back'. The 15th Vernon-Wall lecture. Leicester: British Psychological Society.

Reason, R. and Frederickson, N. (1996) 'Discrepancy definitions or phonological assessment', in Reid, G. (ed.) *Dimensions of Dyslexia: Assessment, Teaching and the Curriculum*, Vol. 1. Edinburgh: Moray House Publications.

Reid, G. (1986) 'An examination of pupil stress before and after transfer from primary to secondary school'. Unpublished MEd thesis, University of Aberdeen.

Reid, G. (1998) *Dyslexia: A Practitioner's Handbook* (2nd edn). Chichester: Wiley.

Reid, G. (2003) *Dyslexia: A Practitioner's Handbook* (3rd edn). Chichester: Wiley.

Reid, G. and Given, B. K. (1998) 'The interactive observation style identification', in Given, B. K. and Reid, G. (1999) *Learning Styles: A guide for teachers and parents*. St Anne's on Sea: Red Rose Publications.

Reid, G. and Kirk, J. (2001) *Dyslexia in Adults: Education and employment*. Chichester: Wiley.

Reid, G. and Wearmouth, J. (2002) 'Issues for assessment and planning of teaching and learning', in Reid, G. and Wearmouth, J. (eds) *Dyslexia and Literacy: Theory and Practice*. Chichester: Wiley.

Richardson (2002) 'Dyslexia, dyspraxia and ADHD: Can nutrition help?'. Paper presented at the Eighth Cambridge Conference, Helen Arkell Dyslexia Centre, March.

Riding, R. and Rayner, S. (1998) *Cognitive Styles and Learning Strategies: Understanding style differences in learning and behaviour*. London: David Fulton Publishers.

Robertson, J. (1997) 'Neuropsychological intervention in dyslexia'. Paper presented at the 25th Anniversary Conference of the British Dyslexia Association.

Schoss, D. (2001). Personal communication.

Singleton, C. (2002) 'Dyslexia: cognitive factors and implications for literacy', in Reid, G. and Wearmouth, J. (eds) *Dyslexia and Literacy: Theory and Practice*. Chichester: Wiley.

Smythe, I. (1997) 'World Dyslexia Network Foundation', in *The International Book of Dyslexia*. London; World Dyslexia Network Foundation, PO Box 3333, London.

Snowling, M. J. (2000) *Dyslexia*. (2nd edn). Oxford: Blackwell.

Stein, J. F. (1995) 'A visual defect in dyslexia?', in Nicolson, R. I. and Fawcett, A. J. (eds) *Dyslexia in Children: Multidisciplinary perspectives.* Hemel Hempstead: Harvester Wheatsheaf.

Stein, J. F. (2000) 'Genetic studies in dyslexia'. Paper presented at the BDA Training for Trainers Conference, Manchester, May.

Stein, J. F. (2002) 'The sensory basis of reading'. Paper presented at the Eighth Cambridge Conference, Helen Arkell Dyslexia Centre, March.

Task Force on Dyslexia (2001). Report of Dublin Government. Publications. Available online at http://www.irlgov.ie/educ/pub.htm

Tod, J. and Fairman, A. (2001) 'Individualised learning in group settings', in Peer, L. and Reid, G. *Dyslexia: Successful Inclusion in the Secondary School.* London: David Fulton Publishers.

Tunmer, W. E. and Chapman, J. (1996) 'A developmental model of dyslexia: Can the construct be saved?' *Dyslexia*, **2**(3), November, 179–89.

Weedon, C. and Reid, G. (2001) *Listening and Literacy Index.* London: Hodder and Stoughton.

Weedon, C. and Reid, G. (2003) *Special Needs Assessment Portfolio.* London: Hodder and Stoughton.

West, T. G. (1997) *In the Mind's Eye.* Buffalo, NY: Prometheus Books.

Wilkins, A. J. (1995) *Visual Stress.* Oxford: Oxford University Press.

Wilson, J. (1993) Phonological Awareness Training Programme. London: University College London, Educational Psychology Publishing.

Witkin, H. and Goodenough, D. (1981) 'Cognitive styles: essence and origins', *Psychological Issues Monograph*, 51. New York: International Universities Press.

Wolf, M. (1991) 'Naming speed and reading: the contribution of the cognitive neurosciences', *Reading Research Quarterly*, **26**, 123–41.

Wolf, M. (1996) 'The double deficit hypothesis for developmental dyslexics'. Paper read at the 47th Annual Conference of the Orton Dyslexia Conference, Boston, MA.

Wolf, M. and O'Brien, B. (2001) 'On issues of time, fluency and intervention', in A. Fawcett (ed.) *Dyslexia, Theory and Good Practice.* London: Whurr.

Wray, D. (1994) *Literacy and Awareness.* London: Hodder and Stoughton.

Index